YOUR PAIN

IS CHANGING YOU

YOUR PAIN
IS CHANGING YOU

DISCOVER THE POWER OF
A GODLY RESPONSE

DAVID CROSBY

NEW HOPE
PUBLISHERS
Gospel-Centered. Missions-Driven.

BIRMINGHAM, ALABAMA

New Hope® Publishers
PO Box 12065
Birmingham, AL 35202-2065
NewHopeDigital.com
New Hope Publishers is a division of WMU®.

Library of Congress Cataloging-in-Publication Data

Crosby, David, 1953-
    Your pain is changing you : discover the power of a Godly response / by David Crosby.
    pages cm
     ISBN 978-1-59669-413-2 (sc)
     1. Pain—Religious aspects—Christianity. 2. Suffering—Religious aspects—Christianity. 3. Consolation. I. Title.
     BV4909.C77 2014
     248.8'6—dc23
                    2014013611

Cover design: MTW Studios
Interior design: Glynese Northam

ISBN-10: 1-59669-413-0
ISBN-13: 978-1-59669-413-2

N144119 • 0814 • 3M1

DEDICATION

For my father, *Russell Bryan Crosby*,

    whose vibrant faith was passed on as a living flame to his children,

    who endured all his pain through the balm of God's presence,

    who managed to love, sometimes dangerously,

    whose death left me longing for another conversation.

CONTENTS

ACKNOWLEDGMENTS

I have always felt like one of the church members even though I was the pastor. As a member of the church, I have felt the loving concern of hundreds of people through these years. Kind and caring people have traveled with me through life's difficulties, sat with me in my sorrow, embraced me in my pain, and prayed for me when all words failed.

I acknowledge the heroes of my faith—skilled business leaders who shepherded me as their friend, coffee-drinking buddies who met me weekly to chew the fat, elderly women who prayed for me when they were dying, children who never even saw my faults but loved me as if I were the gold standard for pastors.

Ordinary people with sturdy faith and hearts of love have carried me forward throughout my life. I feel their hugs every day. I am buoyed by their prayers and often surprised by their continuing affection for me even when my shortcomings are painfully obvious.

I think of aged friends like Cora Webb who took me under her wing and taught me as her 21-year-old pastor, and Betsy Murphy who prayed for me from the bed where she was confined.

Businessmen like Charlie Wise, Richard Adkerson, and Drayton McLane Jr., befriended me, encouraged me, invited me into their lives, and showed me a glimpse of their world.

Joe McKeever is the person I call when I just have to talk to somebody. Travis Bundrick picks up when I ring even though he knows I want free advice.

My siblings Timothy, Thomas, and Daniel, closest to my age, hear from me and listen patiently when I am happy or struggling. I process everything out loud with my dear wife, Janet, and her counsel keeps me on track.

My daughter, Rebekah, chooses a transparent life despite its complications, and shares her feelings more honestly than anyone I know. She is the heroine in a tale of indescribable pain and prayer, and she is allowing me to tell her story yet again. I am so grateful that her baby, Graham, survived the accident. He leaps from his mother's arms into mine.

And I leap into God's.

LIFE IN A TROUBLED WORLD

(INTRODUCTION TO CHAOS AND CARNAGE)

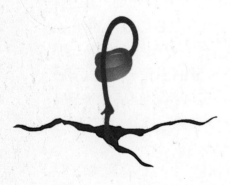

His big brother characterized him as a professional thief, which seemed to clear up some questions about why the boy was inside someone else's yard when the gate was locked. It was past midnight, after all—and who climbs over the fence that time of night intending to do good?

The homeowner later tried to explain that he was simply protecting his wife and child. Year by year, New Orleans has had the highest homicide rate in the nation. Many people, criminal and non, own weapons for that very reason. This young father appeared to be, like so many, frightened that the terror outside his gate would one day creep inside.

According to media reports, the would-be thief "made a move," and the father discharged his weapon, striking the intruder in the head.

And that was that—another teenage boy hit the ground in a city that hears and sees them fall every day.

I read the long account in the *Times-Picayune* start to finish and shook my head as I slowly lowered the newspaper and rested my hands on the kitchen table.

It took me back, that story did, like so many stories do in this "city that care forgot." I wrote these stories once upon a time. Thirty years ago I worked the crime scenes as a cub reporter, displaying my journalistic credentials around my neck with the hope they would protect me as loud and sometimes disorderly people gathered to survey bodies lying askew in the streets. I scratched out the facts standing under street lamps, notebook in hand, and interviewed law enforcement personnel and people in the crowd who seemed especially disturbed by the killings.

Journalists can become jaded. They see so much of the ugly side of life. A religion editor, secular and loud in his own convictions, gave me a gift one Easter—a penciled picture of a rabbit crucified on a cross. When trouble is all you see most days, tragedy and comedy combine to create a truly macabre view of the world.

Two murders from my days as a reporter in New Orleans came to mind as I laid down the newspaper and removed my reading glasses. The first homicide I covered for the newspaper happened in front of the Hyatt Regency next to the Superdome. I arrived at the scene just after the police and found a body sprawled in the gutter, a pool of blood around his head. He was a history professor from New Jersey. The shooter was a 14-year-old who demanded his wallet. The shooter went to prison for three decades.

The second murder that came to mind is one that perpetually rests just on the surface of my subconscious since the day I saw the crime scene. The seminary where I lived with my wife and children and where I was training to be a pastor was only a couple of miles north of the address they handed me as I left the newsroom that night.

I arrived this time with a crowd already gathered up and down the street. I pulled out my badge to make sure it was visible and walked on the very crown of the road toward the commotion two blocks away. Single-story shotgun houses and doubles with camelbacks, all narrow and deep, crowded the sidewalks on both sides. The body was spread-eagle in a tiny yard under the glow of a single noisy streetlight just tripped on by the gathering darkness.

This was one of the few times that I was afraid for my own safety at a crime scene. I felt this same way at a triple murder in the Irish Channel late one night, a drug deal gone bad. The coroner's wagon was there, too, but the bodies were in black plastic bags as they loaded them.

This victim, a 14-year-old boy, was lying as he died with his face in the grass, feet toward the street, shoe soles up, legs apart, his arms twisted slightly and stretched out both ways. A New Orleans Police Department officer in uniform was going through the boy's pockets but not yet moving the body.

Satisfied that he had emptied the contents of his pockets, the officer stood up slowly, turned, and walked across the street near where I was standing. A woman beside me was wailing in anguish. She was propped upright by unknown persons supporting her elbows and shoulders. She would surely have collapsed without them. The officer indicated that he wanted to give her the pockets' contents. She cupped her trembling hands in front of her, and the officer poured a few coins and trinkets into them.

Her knees buckled, and her weight sagged on the arms of those who held her. She threw back her face and looked to heaven and cried, "My son! My son!" The words echoed up and down the street and shocked it into silence.

Officers loaded the body in the coroner's wagon near where the woman stood, and it motored away, leaving her standing in the street weeping, still propped up by her neighbors. I learned later that she was a widow. The victim, who was playing football in the street with his buddies, was shot in the back with a .22-gauge rifle by a man sitting on his porch. The victim was his mother's only child.

I tell people, even the editorial staff at the newspaper, that I came back to New Orleans as a pastor to spread the good news, not the bad news. I prefer my new assignment, sharing the good news amidst the troubles and trials of urban life. I tell the church members that I want them to "shine like stars in the universe" as they "hold out the word of life" (Philippians 2:15).

These teenage boys, killing and being killed, trouble my sleep and my sermons. We work every day to make a difference in their lives. The leading cause of death among them is murder. They live in a world that I have never lived in and cannot even imagine. I tell them about Christ Jesus and His love. I baptize them. I see them in prison and attend their funerals.

A young man was gunned down in Central City. His body was riddled with bullets. Family members and friends were holding a repast (life celebration) for him at Taylor Playground, a public park where we were conducting worship services outdoors and feeding people and teaching children.

Our church took a busload of children to the park that evening. They arrived to find it full of people in matching T-shirts with the dead man's picture emblazoned on the front and the name of his gang on each sleeve. Instead of dates for birth and death, the T-shirts read, "Thugged in" and "Thugged out" with his birthday and death day etched beside this startling nomenclature. Those are some mighty discouraging parentheses for time on the planet.

Do we who identify ourselves with the name of Jesus really have good news for people who truly feel—and maybe are—

thugged in and thugged out of this world? We believe so, but those who are thugged in and out only stop to listen when they see that we have "skin in the game." It is a harsh and frightening daily existence for them, a struggle to survive, and easy platitudes mean nothing. Their mothers pray that they will make it to graduation without getting shot and that they will do well enough in school to go to college and get out of the line of fire.

Our church began a partnership with John Dibert Community School five years ago. We provide uniforms for children whose families cannot afford them. We host a breakfast for parents and send volunteers to help with festivals and other school activities. Members of our church help tutor children at the school. Each Friday we bring backpacks filled with child-friendly food items to send home with kids who display signs of hunger on Monday mornings. Many children in our city's schools are at risk of hunger over the weekends.

Brandajah attended kindergarten at John Dibert. One day she asked her kindergarten teacher, a member of my congregation, if heaven was real. "Yes, Brandajah," the teacher told her. "Heaven is real." But the teacher wondered about the question. Brandajah asked other authority figures in her life about death and dying, and about heaven. She really wanted to know if heaven is real, an unusual curiosity for a child so young. School officials at John Dibert Community School became deeply concerned about her condition and environs at home. They assigned someone to watch Brandajah during the school day. They called the Louisiana Department of Child and Family Services a dozen times that school year reporting that Brandajah showed signs of sexual and physical abuse. Nothing changed for Brandajah. She was trapped in a place I cannot describe or imagine.

Brandajah was left alone in her home. Her mother locked her in a bedroom and left to take care of some business. Brandajah found a loaded pistol in that bedroom where her mother locked her up. Her mother said she knew that the homeowner, a known felon, kept the gun in that room. I don't know what happened. Police say Brandajah's forehead had powder burns on it as if she pressed the barrel against her skin and pulled the trigger. People who knew this little girl are deeply troubled. They think it likely, disturbing as the thought may be, that Brandajah saw that loaded gun as a way out of hell and into heaven.

Somebody please help me understand how individuals and communities allow children to live in such misery. Surely this sorrow is shared by us all.

EVERYONE HURTS SOMETIMES

I have known some personal suffering. My father died when he reached 80 years of age. I miss him terribly. My wife, Janet, had a malignant tumor removed. I worry sometimes her cancer will recur. Our smallest grandchild, Graham, spent ten days in ICU (intensive care unit) hanging between life and death. That was by far the most frightening journey of my life. I am still reeling from it.

I tried to give leadership through the relocation of First Baptist New Orleans, a herculean effort on the part of many people that expended the resources and energy of our church family and cost us emotionally in ways that are hard to quantify or describe or even contemplate.

No sooner had we gotten it done and settled into the new facility than Hurricane Katrina came charging through, dealing death and destruction in every quarter. Her winds tore the new skin off the building. Rainwater flooded in on the east and north and managed to damage all parts of the buildings in some way. Then a sweltering heat trapped the new facility in high humidity for five weeks. The ticket to fix it was $3 million and change. We lost 700 people permanently, and the community to which we relocated may never again have the population it contained when we moved.

We worked like Trojans day and night and suspended normal ministry programming so we could help our community dig out of the debris. We scratched and clawed our way back to even, with the help of thousands, and learned to love our city in a new way.

In the meantime, we helped one another restore our personal lives and properties. Both of my daughters lost their homes, and their families stayed with us for a while. Others came and went through our home, and we were delighted to be able to accommodate them in their need as others did for us.

We all know suffering that is palpable and deep and sometimes draws us toward the pit of hopelessness. Suicide as a final solution to pain touches every demographic group, rich and poor, black and white, young and old. We saw a lot of self-destruction after Hurricane Katrina. The obituary pages seemed unusually long. And most deaths, even the ones that looked inevitable, we connected to the strains and struggles of the great storm. I buried a 90-year-old man and remember his son shaking his head and saying, "He'd still be alive if they hadn't laid him on that bridge for two days. He just never got over it."

Suffering is not distributed evenly, either in a single person's history or among human lives past or present. My personal sorrows and troubles pale in comparison to the daily plight of others in our community. When our troubles seem few and good things come our way, we say that we are blessed and attribute the good things to God's mercy, mysterious and undeserved. This is proper and a way of acknowledging that tomorrow's storm may strike us dead on and flatten everything we hold dear. People often comment in jest when they have a narrow miss or sink a difficult putt, "I've been living right." Everyone laughs because we know that accidents happen to us all, good and bad. Our moral character does not eliminate us as tornado victims nor make us the best putters in the world.

I do not know why some people suffer so terribly. My friend James is more like Job of the Old Testament than anybody I know. He lost a child in an accident. A second child ended up in prison and a third fell into despair and committed suicide. James lost his health and his mobility. I cannot say why I bounce giggly grandchildren on my knee while James takes bouquets to the cemetery. This is a mystery to me. I think only God knows the answer to why, and He has not told us.

God became man in Jesus of Nazareth. Jesus lived to age 33, was arrested, unjustly convicted, beaten, and nailed to a cross. This terrible event does not tell us why people suffer, but it does show us that God is with us in our suffering.

Jesus took into His heart all the sin and shame and guilt and pain of this world when He hung upon the Cross. His pure heart was burdened with the sickness of the human race. He descended into the abyss holding our sin tightly. That is how He died.

No one can accuse God of standing aloof while we writhe in pain. The Father in heaven saw His own Son die. This is the indisputable demonstration of the love of God (Romans 5:8). We know that God has acted to rescue us from our sin. We know that God has prepared a place for us where there is no pain or sorrow or tears or death. We know that suffering is not God's ultimate purpose for us.

God acted. He did something to rescue us. This is how He responded to suffering.

We also act. We respond to suffering. Our responses vary greatly, and they make a huge difference in the quality of our lives and the lives of those we love.

YOUR PAIN IS CHANGING YOU

Pain will come to you, deeper and darker than you ever imagined. Your suffering will be profound. It may be relentless. If not already, you will one day become acquainted with the suffering of mind and body that inevitably happens to humans in this world.

You do not get to choose the events that come your way nor the sorrows that interrupt your life. They will likely be a surprise to you, catching you off guard and unprepared. You may hold your head in your hands and lament your weak condition and wonder what you ought to do.

You are human, made in the image of God. You will choose your attitude and mind-set and lifestyle in the wake of your greatest sorrow and pain. You are a steward, not only of your resources and gifts, but of your limitations and disasters.

Suffering will probe your soul more deeply and expose your true character more fully than all the victories life can bring. You discover both your constitution and your potential when you are called upon to give "the last full measure of devotion" (Abraham Lincoln, Gettysburg Address).

The roll call of faith is not a list of those least troubled or touched by the sufferings of life. On the contrary, the list of the faithful often includes those most beset by unjust treatment and painful ordeals. They are distinguished not by their freedom from pain but by their faithful response in the midst of it.

This, too, will distinguish you in the family of humans. To suffer, that is common to all. To suffer and still keep your composure, your faith, and your smile, that is remarkable. In fact, onlookers will liken you to Jesus of Nazareth if you suffer patiently without complaint. They will note this quality of faith in you, and it will set your light upon a lampstand more surely and more brightly than any other opportunity in your life.

Pain will change you more profoundly than success or good fortune. Suffering shapes your perception of life, your values and priorities, and your goals and dreams.

Your pain is changing you, this is true.

SNAKE IN THE WELL

Our big family moved 500 miles without leaving Texas, from Canutillo to Richland Springs, when I was a freshman in high school in 1967. I was not a happy camper when Dad announced the move. I had friends, including Irma, my girlfriend, and I liked my life the way it was.

Dad insisted on the move. Mom went reluctantly too. She was terribly upset that first night, I remember, crying and saying, "It's the worst move we ever made!" She was standing with her feet in debris in the middle of a small living room with rotten wallpaper peeling off the walls and Sheetrock sagging from the ceiling joists.

The idea Dad had was to make a living farming, but 140 acres of anything in central Texas was not enough to make a living for a family of ten children. We tried, though, by picking pears, planting peanuts, raising chickens, harvesting pecans, and hunting wild turkeys for food. Mom even roasted two armadillos for dinner one night—not my favorite meal.

Dad soon returned to his former professions, teaching in the local school and preaching at the local church. It was for the best, really. He was a better teacher and preacher than he was a farmer. He made ends meet, but the farm was neglected.

A hand-dug water well near the deep-rutted dirt road that ran by the front gate supplied our home and the barn with water. It was open-mouthed, rimmed with rocks, and around 40 feet deep. Hidden in the weeds that grew tall in the valley, it was out of sight and out of mind most of the time.

Then the water became murky, and we all became aware again of our solitary water source. Dad asked people at Locker Baptist Church what to do about the water. Locker was a tiny community with a cemetery and a white wooden church building situated on the northeast side of an intersection between a ribbon of beaten asphalt and a thinner ribbon of rutted dirt. The tiny congregation held a meeting and decided to ask Dad to preach for them, and he did. Then they asked him to become the pastor.

The church members were concerned about the dirty water. They asked Dad if he had treated the well with bleach. He had not, he said, and vowed to treat it as soon as he could secure a gallon of bleach. "Town" to us then was Richland Springs with a population of 300 people, a school, and a couple of stores. Dad bought the bleach there. We all waded through the weeds and went down to the well to see how things would go. We peered into the pit and saw something moving. Dad sent one of his boys back for a flashlight, and soon we discovered a snake was slithering around on the water in the well, maybe 30 feet below our feet. The water was mud-colored, and we were all disgusted that we drank it, but we were also fascinated by the snake and leaned over the well for a long time to get a good look. We had no idea how that snake got in the well.

Dad did not know how to extract the snake from the well. He decided to go ahead and treat the well with the snake still in it. He screwed the top off the plastic jug and poured the whole gallon of bleach into the water below. We never saw the snake again. It makes my stomach flop just to think about what happened to it, but the water soon became so clear we could see the stones at the very bottom. The bleach did the trick. We tried not to think about the snake and drank our clean water with gratitude.

Humans always need water, and getting it almost always causes problems. It's why plumbers make so much money and rain is such a big deal in every human settlement. Water is the perfect illustration of simplicity, a clear liquid that comes down from above, flows over and under rocks, gathers in puddles and ponds, and constitutes most of every human's body weight. We cannot exist without it.

The goodness of God is like water. We cannot live without it, and if we conclude that we came into existence without the goodness of God, then existence itself is a moral perplexity. We go to this well all the time, every day. The goodness of God is a reservoir of strength and wisdom that channels its way through our daily thoughts and our most profound dissertations. It is where we begin and end in our moral reasoning, and where we go multiple times a day to quench the spiritual thirst that builds in our souls.

The snake is in the well, a disturbing symbol of evil that slithers through biblical history and theology from "the serpent deceived me, and I ate" in the Garden of Eden (Genesis 3:13) to "that ancient serpent, who is the devil, or Satan" in Revelation 20:2.

Why is this snake in the well? Why does evil exist in a world created and sustained by a good God? The problem of evil is the most persistent and perplexing puzzle in religious discussion. It clouds the vision like disturbed sediment clouds the water. It makes you pause before you drink and look for a clearer spot somewhere in the pond. Sometimes you move on without the water because the snake is in the well.

COUNTY JAIL

I was standing in a county jail—not my favorite place. This one was built of massive stone blocks, blond-colored and rough-hewn, a rural jail operated by the local sheriff. It was cold and barren, just boxes made of steel and stone with no apparent amenities—no televisions or common spaces for conversation, no recreational room with barbells, no reading room with donated books and magazines. It was stark, I thought.

County jails can be tough places to do time. State facilities are better, and federal ones usually the best. Longer-term incarceration means more organized effort at rehabilitation, more access to continuing education, and more careful inspection for inhumane treatment. Inmates who do all their time in county jails are generally serving shorter sentences. Many are, like Sam, awaiting court dates and eventual moves to state prisons.

I showed up early that day, just after an orange sun peeked over the horizon of plateaus and lit up dew-sprinkled leaves. The drive at dawn was the best part of this trip. I had spied a pair of whitetails just before sunup, edging out of a scrub oak thicket, their damp coats shining in the first dashes of sunshine. I took my foot off the accelerator and watched them for a brief minute, soaking in the beauty of a country morning.

Now I was going through the motions, making good on a promise to my friend. The deputies were cooperative. I was a pastor looking for a prisoner named Sam. They only had a few guys locked up that day, and they knew right away who I was talking about.

A big sigh escaped my lips. My shoulders were hunched like I was carrying the weight of the world. I shook myself and tried out a smile. No need to be glum.

The deputy motioned to me and led the way, hollered to be buzzed in. An invisible attendant pushed a button somewhere, and a lock snapped. I stepped out of the free world into the world where security was always job one.

I always jump a little, involuntarily, when I hear the clang of iron on iron behind me. The cold ring makes me shiver still, even after hundreds of visits to many facilities, most of them much bigger than the one I was in. This place was not well-lit, and it smelled damp. I decided to stand, not sit, while they went to get Sam. I was in a hurry to get out of there, to be honest. After all, what was left to say?

Soon the shuffle of chained feet echoed in a dark corridor in front of me, and a two-man procession emerged, prisoner first, his hands chained too. He was in that orange jumpsuit that prisoners sometimes wear with "Sheriff's Department" emblazoned on the back of his shirt. He looked bleary-eyed, like he hadn't slept much. Jail can be a hard place to sleep.

Sam was older than most inmates, gray-haired and bow-legged with wrinkled hands and squinting eyes. I was there at the request of his brother who was concerned about Sam's eternal destiny—with good reason.

Sam shook my hand, and I introduced myself and told him I knew his brother. He nodded, not surprised. You never know how it will affect a person to have a pastor show up for a visit. Pastors often deliver bad news to inmates, death messages, and such.

The poor man was emotional right from the start, all broken up and heaving big sobs. He guessed why I was there, and he was glad I came. He had a question for me that came out early and remained the centerpiece of our conversation that day. It still surprises me that Sam was so upset about it and that it was on his mind so strongly.

It's not like I had never heard the question. I hear it all the time. It goes through my mind almost every day, prompted by one thing or another.

I just didn't think it would be on his mind. That's the point. But it was. At least, that is where he jumped the minute we started our talk.

He didn't really get into any small talk on the front end. He didn't try to find out who I was or what I knew about him or his criminal record or the Bible or theology. He went straight to talking about little children somewhere in the world who were suffering that very moment. He turned his back on me, lifted his head, and looked at those massive stones in the wall behind him. He wrung his hands and got all choked up over the thought of these unknown children in pain.

And he wanted to know how I knew that God was good.

I asked myself what was going on with this behavior and why this man in such deep trouble was so emotional about these children he'd never seen. But he was insistent and never veered off topic. I thought he deserved my best answer, but I suspected it wouldn't be good enough for him.

How do you know if God is good? The goodness of God may be the fundamental question in this universe chock-full of questions. No question is more central to our overall perspective as humans. You get the picture. If God is good, then this old world we live in begins and ends with goodness: goodness in creation and goodness in completion. If God is not good—or not there at all—then the quality of our beginning and our end is shrouded in moral darkness and ultimate irrelevance.

I first learned the importance of this question from a medical doctor, Doctor Dan, who told me that his whole world changed when he discovered that God was good. He told his story often and with passion. It really was the truth that changed his life. He died, of course, but too young, in his 40s, of a brain cancer that took him stage by stage from brilliant, caring human being to a thin corpse in a fancy box.

No easy answers out there—you've got to learn. The minute you get cocky about what you think you know, you get slammed in the blind spot. And you do have a blind spot. Everybody does. You study the library of what you think you know, and ask yourself what's not there. Nobody's mental library is anywhere near complete—all kinds of holes. You don't even possess the vocabulary to articulate the questions, let alone know the answers. That is the human condition. We are wondrously made, magnificently designed with intellect, emotion, and will. And we are surprisingly limited in our comprehension of the most basic events that come our way.

I learned that morning in jail that Sam was suspicious. He

didn't believe the claims about the goodness of God. Sam suspected that God was not good, though he couldn't be sure. The suffering of children, he said, made him doubt God. He blubbered and wailed about it, like he had lost his last hope, and he was delivering the news to me. I didn't hear or feel any anger in his tears. Mostly it all felt like disappointment, grief, and resignation, like he had been sentenced to live out his days in a world where pain was everywhere and nothing made sense.

I could not console him. He didn't bark at me or push me away. He didn't accuse me or blame me, but he didn't look at me either. Gravity pulled the tears down his cheeks, through the stubble of his beard, and off the tip of his chin. He didn't bother to wipe them away. They seemed like a permanent part of his visage.

They are permanent to me, those tears, because I never saw Sam again. It's how I remember him to this day, rendered almost inarticulate by sorrow, his face wet with tears, looking up and then down, pacing in front of that stone wall.

He let me pray with him before I left. I fumbled for words, stumbled through that prayer. You would think I could pray on autopilot, as much as I do it, but that morning I couldn't collect my thoughts. I was all over the place.

Prayer for me is personal. I try to avoid mumbling memorized phrases strung together for the occasion. When I pray, I want to talk to God, not just perform a religious ritual. People don't realize how hard it is sometimes to formulate a prayer that makes sense and fits the occasion.

I really had no words that morning. I don't know what I uttered. It is part of the reason I remember the encounter so vividly. I felt trapped myself, not by argument or circumstance. I had heard the arguments before. I had often visited people in similar circumstances. I was pinned to the stone wall that day by the crush of disappointment and the agony of despair.

We must acknowledge the genuine human emotion that accompanies the loss of faith and hope. An atheist challenged me in a public setting one day. I was the guest speaker at a meeting of the local chapter of the Secular Humanist Society. He stood up after my presentation, which caused quite a stir, and read to me Psalm 14:1 as if it were written just for him: "The fool says in his heart, 'There is no God.' They are corrupt, their deeds are vile; there is no one who does good."

He felt singled out by the text of Scripture and consigned to being corrupt and vile, living in a place where no one does good. He took the passage personally, as if it were a judgment against him as an atheist along with others of his persuasion. He felt that discrimination against atheists, the assumption that they were evil in behavior, was rooted in this passage.

The man had a story, though I did not know it. Virtually all of the atheists, agnostics, and secularists in the room had at one time believed in God or engaged in religious practice. He spoke sincerely, I felt, and as one who had left behind something precious.

I pointed out to the man that the passage is used by the Apostle Paul in Romans 3 to describe the plight of all people and that the psalm itself declares, "The LORD looks down from heaven on all mankind to see if there are any who understand, any who seek God. All have turned away, all have become corrupt; there is no one who does good, not even one" (Psalm

14:2–3). We are all indicted by Scripture. We all sometimes think and act as if "there is no God." We whisper it in our hearts when our way is not his way, when no one else can hear.

The atheist seemed to understand the broader scope of the passage, but he sunk to his chair unsatisfied, still looking like one especially cursed.

The absence of God and the absence of good are linked in this psalm. The Lord above looks down upon us to see if anyone really understands or seeks Him. The Lord seeks a seeker, and He finds none. He also finds no one truly doing good.

Sam linked these two in his mind as well—the absence of God and the absence of good. But he did it backward. He concluded, reluctantly it seemed to me, that there was no good. Therefore, there was no God. The folly of this is self-evident. "There is no God" means there is no genuine good—not ultimately, not transcendent good. The fool may content himself with what he would describe as good—good food, good clothes, and good company. But banishing God also means banishing true purpose in this world. And goodness without purpose, good without reason, is truly us just fooling ourselves, making up something to calm the panic and disguise the despair and occupy our time on the way to oblivion.

That is what Sam was feeling so deeply and painfully that morning. He was feeling the unmitigated pain and incurable chaos of a world without the "God who works in you to will and to act in order to fulfill his good purpose" (Philippians 2:13).

PEOPLE MAKE CHOICES

But that was not all. I have not told you the whole story. You need to know why Sam was in that jail. His brother, Toby, a good friend, had given me in broad strokes the sad story of Sam's life. We were coffee-drinking buddies, Toby and I, and he was part of the flock, a church member who was well-respected and widely known. We often met at Mona's Coffee Shop, a small drugstore with a watering hole the locals frequented. Mona's decor was 1950s all the way—chrome and plastic swiveling stools at the soda fountain with a half dozen matching booths along the wall.

Usually the conversation was light and cheerful, even when the undertakers joined us. They were full of jokes, those men dressed in dark suits who dealt with death every day, and surprisingly cheerful. They spoke in deep voices with measured, rhythmic tones like human metronomes.

I was a newcomer to the crew in the booths at the back of the drugstore, but I became one of them by trapping them in their own devices. One morning a funeral director told a joke about Oral Roberts. Everybody laughed except me. They noticed and looked my way, feeling me out, and I informed them quietly that Oral had just died. They were understandably apologetic and said they would never have been joking about him if they knew of his demise. I waved it aside with true pastoral grace, sipping my coffee with elbows on the table, waiting for one of them to ask the inevitable question.

"So what happened to him?" asked Rick with practiced sympathy and deep concern. I raised my head slowly and said, "He was out walking his duck and got run over by a motorboat," and went back to my coffee. A moment of silence was followed by a volley of protests and feeble efforts at recovery. That was the day they let me in, including Toby, the elder in the group, and not an undertaker.

Toby had worked through his own difficulties, first in his family of origin, and then with his wife and children. Life had pummeled him into a fine human being focused on helping others. He had surrendered the grand dreams and settled into a routine of service, deeply fulfilled but tentative in criticism and praise.

Square-jawed and square-built, Toby took early retirement from state employment. He continued to do contract services and worked at his own pace. His favored activities were all about children. Most recently he had launched an effort to open a home for troubled kids. The community was frightened by the proposal and killed that dream. But Toby was used to losing as well as winning. He took it in stride and went on to his next project. I really liked him, and he liked me.

FOUR-WAY STOP

Telling me about his brother was like opening an old trunk full of long-held family secrets. To learn about Sam's situation was also to learn about Toby. He wanted me to visit his brother in jail, and he wanted to tell me part of his own story, hard as it was.

Toby's alcoholism was learned behavior, something passed on from his dad who was a violent drunk. Sam took refuge in the bottle as well. These two brothers grew up in the same home with the same parents. Both became alcoholics like their father before them. Somehow their paths diverged. Toby found sobriety through faith in God. His story was all about God's amazing forgiveness and restoration. His marriage was now sweet and tender, and his heart was turned to helping children in need.

Sam, too, was focused on children, but not to help them. Rather, the suffering of children, needless as it seemed to him, hurt him like a knife in his heart. Surely the pain of his own boyhood was part of that disillusionment, and maybe, too, the pain of his own children now separated from their father.

Sam never discovered a place of faith and hope, though people who cared tried to lead him there. His life careened through a series of misfortunes and poor decisions until he fell at last into the heap of despair and gloom I found in the jail that day, unraveled, unrepentant, and unforgiven.

The suffering of children was not some far-off reality to Sam. He was living in the nightmare of his own creation, blaming God for the blow he himself had delivered to innocent children. I could not fathom it. I still find it hard to believe, but the children Sam was so concerned about must surely have been the three little ones that he left fatherless. At a four-way stop on a dark night in the middle of nowhere, Sam never put his foot on the brake. He was so drunk I suppose he never saw the stop sign. He went through the intersection going fast and killed a young father on the way home to his three kids.

The entire time that Sam was talking to me in the jail that day, his crime was in the back of my mind. No, I'd say it was in the front of my mind, even right there between us, like a filter straining his words. I can see him now, going on and on about suffering in the world, pacing up and down along the rock wall like he was trapped in his own mind.

I was struggling with our conversation, wondering if I should point out the obvious. He would not look me in the eye. He looked past me. He surveyed the stones again and again. After our first greeting, his eyes were somewhere else, not on mine.

He was thinking about it, too, his crime. When he held his head in his hands and closed his eyes, he saw the scene of that crash. He was trying to move somewhere else, trying to talk around it, but he saw it and heard it. That was why he tugged on his ears nervously, his hands patting around his head and neck, shaky fingers running through his thin hair. He was hearing and seeing the horror of those fateful seconds again and again. He hung his head and stared at the concrete floor, hoping it would go away, but it never left him.

When Sam lamented the pain in the world, he was remembering bits and pieces of that night on the road. He never said a word about it, but it was there. He was drunk that night, but he was not unconscious. He did not plan to reach that intersection just when the young father took his foot off the brake and put it on the accelerator. Maybe that intersection was completely clear the last time Sam focused his eyes ahead. He was telling himself that the car came out of nowhere. He was arguing that no traffic engineer in his right mind would put a four-way stop at that particular location.

He must have been passing judgment on other humans, not just on God. The people who built the vehicles and serviced the brakes and adjusted the headlights and designed the seat belts and airbags and chose the weight of the steel—all these people must have been targets.

After all, if you are not confessing, you are usually accusing.

I am a pastor, and people often confess their sins to me. They pull me aside to the wall or the window, check both ways, and then describe in two minutes the deepest stain on their souls. You would expect that. I have heard it all, as they say. There is nothing new under the sun. People know that their confessions to me are confidential, that I will not share them with anyone. They know that they can unload and "get if off their chest," that they are in a safe place when they talk to me.

Sam never talked to me about his vehicular homicide that left three children without their dad for the rest of their lives. He did not confess to me at all. I heard no lament from him about his own mistakes, miscalculations, errors of judgment, poor choices, or moral failures. I heard only that God could not be good because innocent children suffered in this world.

Sam accused God. He probably accused other people. Maybe he accused himself. But I never heard it, except between the lines. It puzzled me, his rant against God. I was thinking the whole time Sam was talking, *How can this man accuse God of evil when he just killed a father on his way home to his kids?* Maybe Sam was hiding comfortably behind his good intentions. You have to feel like you possess some high ground morally to accuse the Creator God of being evil. Maybe Sam's high ground was his good intentions.

Sam would not call it "hiding," of course. His intentions being what they were that night, pure as the driven snow, he had no reason to hide. For some people, good intentions are enough to get them off the hook, no matter what they have done. It was truly an accident, Sam would surely argue. Every day thousands of drivers who would spike a Breathalyzer through the roof dribble home without incident. It was the confluence of two key events that the humans involved never imagined would meet: Sam's drunken drive and the father's nightly commute. Additionally, other random details involving rate of speed and mass of materials had to come together in perfect sequence for the father to die. The timing of it had to be precise from the moment when Sam slid behind the wheel and the father climbed into his car right up to the point where their vehicles collided.

The crushing impact of speeding steel had to occur not only at the right moment but at a particular position in the intersection. Only then would the collision be fatal for the dad. A million details came together to kill the man. Only God could have orchestrated it, if it was orchestrated at all. This would explain Sam's insistent anger at God.

But it does not explain why he never mentioned the accident to me. An innocent man who truly believed himself to be the victim of circumstances beyond his control might have started with the lament that a young father had died. He might have mentioned his grief and sorrow, seeing that he was behind the wheel.

The subject of our conversation should have been the incident that landed Sam in jail. It had happened only days earlier. My coming was probably his first opportunity to process this disturbing event with a pastor.

He was silent about the accident because he felt shame or guilt. That is what I think.

I thought about throwing it out there: "Sam, tell me about what happened." But he had ample opportunity to start that conversation and chose not to do so. He had found a comfortable intellectual hideout by questioning the character of God and His design for the world. Sam did not intend to hurt anyone, so the death of the father had moral relevance only regarding the character of God.

Telling yourself that you have good intentions, or that your intentions were not bad, is a way of insisting that you yourself are good. Your intentions reflect the true condition of your inner being, of your heart. If your intentions are good, if you do not intend to harm, then you are fundamentally good.

So what did Sam intend to do that night? He intended to drive his car home safely. He failed to do so. Whose fault was that?

Here is the thing about intentions: nobody really knows what you actually intended to do, sometimes even yourself. Intentions are secrets of the heart. Sam probably did not intend to hurt anyone that night, but he likely did intend to break the law. Maybe he intended to avoid what had happened to him three times before—being stopped by law enforcement officials for driving while intoxicated. Maybe he had enough awareness to know that he was running a stop sign.

Every human action has some unintended consequences. Some human actions are full of unintended consequences. If you shoot a bullet into a crowd, you may not intend to harm anyone, but you are likely to do so anyway.

Somebody said that "the road to hell is paved with good intentions." Sam looked like he was on that road to hell. I think he himself had paved it with what he might call good intentions.

The Word of God is alive and active, according to the Book of Hebrews 4:12: "It judges the thoughts and attitudes of the heart." God knows our intentions. Exposure to God's Word will help us understand how we think—our motives and our intentions. The better we know our own hearts, the less likely we are to accuse God of evil.

RESPONSE-ABILITY

An elephant was in the jail, but neither Sam nor I mentioned it. We conversed for some time without even a hint of the elephant.

No one is responsible for an accident, right, especially a good person who has no intention to harm another?

The absence of intention to harm did not absolve Sam of his responsibility, and both of us knew it. We live in a complex world of action and reaction. Humans have amazing abilities and great powers in this world. They are conscious of their existence. They think about the nature of being and the consequences of choices.

We are enabled by our Creator to respond in a variety of ways to life's pressures and temptations. This volition, or free will, this ability to choose is fundamental to being human, to our doctrine of man. We do not believe that we are robots, preprogrammed from beginning to end. We confess that God is sovereign and that humans are free, and we work all our lives to keep these truths in proper tension with one another. To resolve the tension is to become a heretic, confessing either that God is not sovereign or that humans are not free moral agents.

Even our doctrine of love requires this tension to exist. God loves us freely, not because He is mandated to do so. He gives his love to us freely, and we are to give freely to others. Love is commanded, but it is not coerced. Love must be free to be real. The summary commands of our faith—love God and love others—demand something from us that we must freely give. This mystery is resolved only in the love of God, the first, the perfect, and the prototypical love.

Most all humans agree that it is morally good to relieve suffering and morally evil to needlessly inflict it. Our laws reflect this truth. Jesus Himself acknowledged it in His reformulation of what we know as the Golden Rule: "Do to others as you would have them do to you" (Luke 6:31). The Apostle Paul was most explicit: "Love does no harm to a neighbor. Therefore love is the fulfillment of the law" (Romans 13:10). One dimension of love is the resolve to do no harm.

Yet we do harm ourselves and others all the time. We often inflict harm deliberately. We say things intending to damage others or wound them with our words. We do things in retaliation for wrongs received, returning evil with evil. We feel justified in dealing others harm when they have harmed us.

The harm we do to others is not always as direct as sharp words or deliberate blows. We may harm others by deceiving them or defrauding them. We take what is theirs.

We may hide these blows and wounds in a variety of ways. Neglect is one such hiding place. Through neglect we may deliver even a deathblow without feeling particularly guilty. We often claim to love those whom we harm by neglect. We should remember the words of Pastor James: "If anyone, then, knows the good they ought to do and doesn't do it, it is sin for them" (James 4:17).

The levees that protected New Orleans were manmade features on our planet. Humans drew up a plan to protect our community. They captured the Mississippi River inside mounds of earth and channeled it to a specific place in the Gulf of Mexico. They created similar mounds of earth and concrete along canals and the lakefront of Lake Pontchartrain. They built these barriers to certain specifications expecting that they would protect the people and property within them.

But they failed to do so. The concrete levees along the outfall canals gave way in the great storm. Even the term *natural disaster* is rejected by some people who see the destruction of New Orleans strictly as a manmade disaster, and they hold responsible the US Army Corps of Engineers.

If the engineers who work for the Corps should stand up together and take responsibility for the failure of the levees, they would be saying that they were responsible for the deaths of hundreds of people and the destruction of $100 billion in property and infrastructure. Such an admission is not forthcoming, I expect, though it is not an unreasonable conclusion.

Engineers might argue that God made Hurricane Katrina and set it on a course to New Orleans, and therefore what followed was a natural disaster. It was the most powerful storm ever to strike the American coast, the kind of storm that hits once every 500 years.

Sam might reason that only God could bring events together to cause the death of the young father. People more inebriated than he was that night regularly arrive home safely. The cause of the fatal crash was not his drunkenness but the timing involved. It was an "act of God."

God is the Creator. Everything that happens on this planet is His doing. That's how some people see it. They conclude one of two things: (1) God is not good and has created the evil in the world, Sam's conclusion, or (2) there is no real evil in the world because everything ultimately works out to be good, including what we would call untimely or premature deaths.

Humans are at least in part responsible for some of the trouble that comes upon them. Sometimes they are completely and fully responsible and they admit it. Sometimes they are fully responsible and do not admit it. Blaming God is a common ploy among humans to avoid responsibility for their actions.

We act with nobility and honesty when we take responsibility for our actions and our neglect. We are cowardly when we refuse to do so. Sam never mentioned his own sin in our conversation. This silence indicated to me that he was hiding from an obvious explanation for some of the suffering in the world.

At least three children in this world suffered terribly at the hands of Sam, not at the hands of God, it seems to me. Sam's poor choices and his lawbreaking robbed them of their father. He did what he should not have done and what the law prohibits, driving drunk, and the unthinkable happened as it often does. These consequences, though not intended by Sam, were foreseeable given his actions. He neglected to care for others and for himself. He paid a terrible price, and the dead father and his family paid even more, robbed of every future moment they might have had together.

People are responsible for their actions. This is the clear teaching of the Bible and the inevitable consequence of free will, a wonderful and terrible gift. People have the power to hurt themselves and others. They may deal unjustly and even violently with one another. People are responsible for much of the suffering in the world, and they should not blame God for it nor question His character, though often they do so.

Looking back, I wonder if I should have initiated the difficult conversation about Sam's sin and its terrible consequences. He was judging God, blaming God for sorrow and pain in the world. He was questioning the goodness of God, the fundamental truth upon which is built all our hopes and faith.

My style has always been to let the sinner identify his own sin. The Bible teaches that all of us are sinners (Romans 3:23). The Bible teaches that our sin ends in death (Romans 6:23). The Holy Spirit is the one who convicts of sin (John 16:8). My perspective about the sin of another person is never as accurate as it should be. If I judge another person on the basis of the sin that is most glaring and obvious to me, I may be completely off point. For instance, the sins of ingratitude, envy, lying, and greed loom large in Scripture and are included in lists of horrendous sins (see 1 Corinthians 5:11; Galatians 5:21; 2 Timothy 3:3; Revelation 21:8). These are not sins that I would have noticed in Sam or thought to mention in my efforts to help him see his guilt.

Humans have the ability to respond to suffering and pain. Our very first response should be the honest acknowledgment of our own participation in the pain of another. Humans are obvious suspects in the question of why there is evil in the world. Instead of accusing God, we should be honestly searching our own hearts.

Our moral failure and the suffering that it causes produce in us guilt and shame. Guilt is both internal and external to us. Sam ran a stop sign. He was guilty of breaking the law, as a criminal court would soon rule. We all have ways of ameliorating the sentence of guilt that comes upon us from others. We ran the stop sign because our situation was a semi-emergency.

More difficult to dismiss is our own guilty conscience. The weight of a guilty conscience can crush a man from the inside out. Avoidance and transference are common ploys in the effort to escape personal guilt and assign fault elsewhere.

Sam sinned in his drunkenness. He was responsible for the ensuing tragedy. His insistence that God was not good should have been an insistence that he himself was not good. He might have acknowledged that sin brings death (Romans 3:23). He could have prayed the prayer of Isaiah, "Woe to me!" (Isaiah 6:5). He could have confessed his sin and repented. Blaming God rather than confessing his sin compounded the alienation that Sam was already experiencing from persons and society.

Human sin and failure do not account for all the evil in the world. The crafty serpent was in the Garden of Eden before our first parents sinned. The tree of the knowledge of good and evil was in the middle of the garden, and it was the source of their temptation. Humans want to be gods, knowing good and evil. The temptation to create our own moral universe, one in which we are supreme arbiter, never goes away. But that is not the whole story to evil in the world.

We should respond with honest acknowledgment of our participation in the cycle of evil. It's a good beginning. But it is one of a whole range of responses that humans make as they see and experience trouble and sorrow.

FIVE-DOLLAR BILL

They thought a clergyman should do it, so the funeral director called for me. He was already at the hospital because the attending physician had called him. Neither the funeral director nor the physician wanted to tell the young woman still lying in the maternity ward that her baby was dead.

I did not relish the thought of delivering this devastating news. But I told all the funeral directors in town that they could call on me if they had need of a pastor. I felt that this situation in general fell within my duties before God and His church. The job of a pastor sometimes involves "death messages," informing people of the death of a loved one. Some people associate the pastor so closely with death that they will go into hysterics when they open the door and see the pastor standing there. One mother grabbed her daughter and began to weep at the very sight of me even though I was there to give her good news. Patients lying in hospital beds waiting for test results sometimes react in a similar fashion.

This woman will be alarmed to see me, I thought to myself as I pulled into the parking lot. *When she hears the word* Reverend *she will start to cry.* I buffed the toes of my shoes on the back of my pant legs, craned up to get a look at myself in the rearview mirror, and patted back to flat a couple of stubborn curls. Time for a haircut.

It was a small, private hospital with only a couple of physicians on site. I knew it was often the choice of people in our community who were economically deprived or had no health insurance. A receptionist greeted me as I stepped into the lobby. A burly young man, skin darkened by the sun, leaned against the wall to my left, gazing out the window. His steel-toed boots were scuffed and stained. His shirt was long-sleeved, blue, and tucked into faded blue jeans held snug by a wide leather belt. His hair was close-cropped, his beard a day-old stubble. His eyes were dark, and he was staring into the sunlight without seeing a thing.

The receptionist pointed to the left. I found the physician and the funeral director conversing in an examination room.

"Oh, hello, Pastor Crosby," the funeral director said, and shook my hand. He always wore a suit with a tie, and always spoke a cheerful word. We had worked together many times.

The physician was nearing retirement age if not already there. He was a short, wide man, bald and sweating profusely, wearing a white coat smudged with blood. I had seen him before but never met him. We introduced ourselves, and he described the situation.

"She had a rugged night of labor. She and the child were in trouble. Finally she gave birth to a baby boy this morning. The baby was alive, but once we cleaned him up he would not stop crying. He died an hour ago; I don't yet know why. The father knows that the baby is dead, but he wants us to tell her."

The funeral director said to me, "I think you should go in and tell her that her baby died. Then I will bring the baby in for her to see and hold, if she would like. She needs to see the baby for herself. It's the only way that she will be certain that her baby is dead."

"OK," I replied, nodding and straightening my spine. "That sounds right. Where is she?"

They directed me across the hall. I stepped into a private room and slowly pushed the curtain back. A large, young woman with a spray of long black hair lay on the bed with a white blanket pulled up under her chin, gripped with both hands, knuckles white. She was showing the strain of a long night of labor without rest and a morning of fear and uncertainty.

I stepped to the side of the bed and introduced myself: "My name is David Crosby. I am a pastor here in town." She nodded her head and listened with concern in her eyes. "The doctor told me that they did everything they could for your baby."

She nodded again. "I heard him crying for hours down the hall, but I didn't know why he just kept crying."

"Your baby has died. I am sorry to have to tell you," I said, and she began to weep.

"I knew something was wrong," she said between sobs.

And the funeral director stepped into the room with the dead baby wrapped in a small, white blanket and cradled in his arm. "Here is your baby," he said. He leaned over toward the mother and pulled the corner of the blanket back to expose the tiny face. "I think you need to see him." He leaned further over the bed and held the baby close to its mother. She pried herself up with one elbow and patted the baby as she cried. She did not try to take the body. The mother's hand fell suddenly to her side, and the funeral director stood upright and lifted the baby away. Without another word, he stepped out of the room.

I took her trembling hand and said a short prayer asking God for comfort and help. She thanked me between sobs and dabbed her nose and eyes with a tissue.

"Would you say a few words over him?" she asked with some hesitation. She was uncertain, I guessed, whether that would be standard practice in this situation. I said that I would. We talked for some time, and I assured her that her baby was with God in heaven. Then I left her alone in the room. I passed through the hospital lobby and noticed that the young man was gone.

He was present, though, two days later, when we gathered at the gravesite, looking in dress and demeanor just as I had seen him at the hospital. The child was his, and he and the mother were husband and wife. This was their first baby. They sat together without any displays of affection or efforts to comfort one another, their baby's coffin right in front of them.

It was a dark day, threatening rain, and the green canopy flapped in a stiff breeze. The funeral director set up a dozen wooden folding chairs under the canopy near the tiny, white casket. Only half were occupied as I moved to the foot of the casket and opened my Bible.

My footing was unsteady. The tarp that covered the ground around the grave also covered ground-level headstones and footstones. Walking was treacherous. I shifted my feet to find level ground and looked toward the funeral director. He gave me the go-ahead, and I read the text of John 14:1–6 (KJV) beginning with, "Let not your heart be troubled." It is my default passage for funerals, particularly when I do not know the family.

I spoke only briefly, assuring them of the love of the Father for them and for their child. I told them about the death of King David's baby and how the king said that he would go to be with the child one day. King David believed that he would "dwell in the house of the Lord forever" (Psalm 23:6). Therefore, I said, he believed that his baby was in the house of the Lord.

"And that is where your baby is also." I quoted the children's song "Jesus Loves Me": "Little ones to him belong." I gripped my Bible tightly and led in a short prayer, closing with the recitation of the Lord's Prayer. A couple of voices murmured through that prayer with me. The entire graveside service took less than ten minutes.

I stepped forward to shake hands with the father who occupied the first chair in the front row. As I stretched out my hand, he stood to his feet suddenly, unsteadily. He thrust out his hand and slapped a wadded piece of paper into mine.

"I wish they had both died," he said without emotion, loud enough for his wife to hear. Then he turned and strode out of the cemetery. I stood there stunned, watching him pick his way through the tombstones with long strides. I worked the paper out of its wad with my thumb and index finger and saw it was a soiled five-dollar bill.

His wife was distraught. She stood up slowly, gripped my arms to steady herself, and wept without words.

I could only guess what was going on in that moment between this bereaved couple. Neither one of them ever shared with me the dynamics of their relationship or anything about their history. I encountered them twice, briefly, and this is the whole story as I experienced it.

It wasn't the whole story for them, of course. They knew each other for at least nine months, probably longer. During the months of her pregnancy they did not grow together. They were two individuals, married but alone.

The wife was sorrowful and full of tears. The husband was angry, resentful, sullen, and bitter. In the end he insulted me in a way few people have. I remember his insult vividly to this very day. And I wish I could return his five-dollar bill. I never wanted it.

Maybe that is all the man thought of pastors and preachers —money-grubbers. Perhaps his insult toward me was really an insult toward God.

His comment and behavior remain inexcusable regardless of any history he may have experienced with his wife. His cruel words and abrupt abandonment of her at the grave of their child had no place in that moment, if they belonged anywhere. He was bereft of all decency and consideration. He displayed no goodness, patience, courage, love, or kindness.

He intended to harm, to hurt, and to wound his wife. He left even me with a scar on my spirit, an awful memory in my mind. Think of what his words and actions did to her then and for the years to come.

These words were premeditated. He prepared them. He discovered the five-dollar bill, removed it from his wallet, and transferred it to the front pocket of his blue jeans before he sat in that cemetery. He resented my presence and the very event of his child's funeral. He scorned his wife and told her so.

He is a crude example of one way that people respond to

pain—they spread it around. If they are going to hurt, then others will hurt with them. If they feel unjustly harmed, then they will harm others unjustly. Cruel things have been said to them and done to them, and they are not content until they do the same to others.

Angry people explode. Sometimes their targets are predictable, sometimes not. When nursed and harbored in the heart, resentment and bitterness break out unexpectedly and lash out indiscriminately.

Maybe the poor woman had harmed her young husband. I doubt it, but no harm done to him could explain or excuse his behavior at the grave. No, I think he was harmed by life itself, resentful of his condition and situation and angry at God.

We do not know why one baby dies and another lives. We cannot fathom the mysteries of life and death, but we do control how we will respond to our losses and our pain. Becoming cruel and harming others is the choice of cowards, thieves, liars, and murderers. We should not want to be numbered with them.

His statement was probably incomplete and inaccurate. Rather than simply wishing his child and wife dead, he likely wished himself dead as well. He was reaping a bitter fruit in his life. He had been hurt by his own choices and the choices of others. His pain went right to the core, and he allowed it to twist him into the monstrous and pathetic human I glimpsed in the cemetery that day.

Sometimes we allow our pain to turn us into angry, bitter people who hurt others, but we do not have to go down that road. We have another option, a truly beautiful way to respond to others even though we are in pain.

CORA'S PRAYER

Mona's Coffee Shop was nearly at capacity when I arrived a little late in the morning. The funeral directors filled one booth, and three of the deacons from my church were in another. I shook hands all around and slipped into the booth beside Toby.

"Two sugars, two creams," I told the waitress, and listened as Blue, another deacon, continued his lament about transmission problems in his new pickup truck.

"Hey, I'll drive you to Georgetown," I offered when he took a breath, knowing he would refuse. Blue fancied himself a comedian, and he had a quick wit.

"Thanks, preacher," he said with an exaggerated drawl, "but I'm not getting in that beat-up Toyota of yours until I've got a current tetanus shot." My Camry was old and dented.

"Did you hear about Cora?" asked Toby, turning my way. "They've got her down at the emergency room. Her heart, I think."

"Better check on that," I said, and threw a dollar on the table to cover my coffee, more or less. Cora was a teacher in our church and a true friend. She suffered from congestive heart failure and had been hospitalized repeatedly in recent months.

I walked in the emergency room entrance a few minutes later, but Cora had been moved upstairs to the intensive care unit (ICU). When I finally found her, I thought she was already dead. She was lying on her back under a white sheet on a small aluminum gurney like the emergency medical teams use. Her hands were folded over her chest, and her eyes were closed.

Nurses were scurrying here and there in the corridor adjacent to ICU, but none were paying attention to her at that moment. I approached the gurney and took a better look. Her hands were small and frail. Her skin was thin and white like paper. I looked and listened, but I could not tell if she was breathing.

She was cold to my touch as I took her hand. She opened her eyes and looked at me. I smiled, and she did, too, a small, forced smile that pinched her eyes closed and pulled back her cheeks and left her lips in a straight line. More like a grimace, I thought, as she wrinkled her brow and clenched her teeth. She was hurting.

She was dear to me, and I did not want to lose her. She was my friend and confidant, and I had prayed with her many times. She was wrinkled with age but retained the bright countenance of a cheerful heart.

I met Cora on my first Sunday at the church. I was wandering from place to place, class to class, taking a look at things and trying to acquaint myself with the structure of our small groups. I opened the classroom door in a far corner of the church facility and saw colorful curtains and area rugs. Two dozen women, mostly elderly, sat in a circle of chairs.

"Good morning, Pastor," said Cora, standing erect behind a small wooden podium with an open Bible lying on it. I returned her greeting and learned that this was the Ruth Class, one of our larger Bible studies.

I surveyed the group again. These ladies had laid claim to their space in all kinds of ways—homemade cushions on their chairs, accent furniture in the corners, knickknacks on the shelves. Posters describing distant missions enterprises were pinned to two bulletin boards along with pictures of missionaries.

I was in a rush that morning, doing my rounds, learning about the church organization, and I failed to fully appreciate either Cora or her class.

Once I made my first visit to Cora's home, however, she was never far from my mind. I could not look at her after that visit without thinking of her two-story frame house and the living room with lumpy stuffed chairs of subdued prints where she gave me glimpses of where she had come from, who she was, and the heart of her long life journey.

She called for me. She asked me to come visit her. I can look like the absent-minded professor, and that must have been my demeanor when we met in her class that day. "He will need prompting," she must have thought, and made a mental note to contact me. She wanted to know me, her pastor, and she wanted to be known. She took the initiative, made the call, and prepared to share with me the story that only her true friends knew.

I found her house near the railroad tracks that ran parallel to the major east-west thoroughfare and passed through down-town. The narrow street was paved with red bricks. Her house sat on the edge of the retail district, nondescript, white paint peeling at the edges. I don't remember any yard, just a shade tree near a dirt driveway that ran up the right side of the house.

Cora answered my knock and invited me in. She was dressed for church on a weekday morning, prepared for her formal visit with the new pastor. I followed her single file through a foyer full of furniture and a dark hallway to the room she lived in—high ceiling, long wall to the north with three small windows.

"Pastor, I am not a widow," she began. I had scarcely settled into the chair opposite hers. She sat back in her chair, relaxed, her head resting on its high back. Her small eyes, set back and bracketed by wrinkles, were hidden behind the glare on her dark-rimmed eyeglasses. Her face was small. Her dentures protruded slightly as she spoke. Her mouth was dry.

I had assumed she was a widow. She lived by herself, apparently, in her big house.

"I married a man I loved. His name is Tom. We were both young. We have been married now for many years. We never had children."

I glanced around the room to see if I had missed some evidence of Tom's presence. I felt that I should respond somehow to this revelation, but I could think of nothing to say. I leaned forward to hear the rest of the story.

"Tom is gone," she said matter-of-factly. "I don't know where he is. Truthfully, I don't know whether he is alive or dead. I have not seen him in several years now." Her voice did not break. She said it without emotion, like talking about the death of a loved one 30 years ago.

I must have stirred in my chair. Maybe my mouth was hanging open. She attended to me. "Would you like a glass of water?"

"That would be good," I replied, and she disappeared for a moment, small heels clicking on the wooden floor. She was strong, self-assured, judging by her gait and her conversation.

An unusual woman, I said to myself. She returned shortly with two glasses of water.

She settled in her chair and took a slow sip of water.

"I have lived by myself for most of our married life," she continued. "Tom disappeared often, without explanation or warning. I never knew where he went. I tried to find him at first, without success, because I was worried." She paused. "I still worry, but there is nothing I can do."

I tried to imagine this painful equilibrium developing in her heart. The light of her dreams had flickered, dimmed, and died. She no longer hoped for a happy marriage. She had long since passed her child-bearing years. She was resigned and adjusted to being alone in the world.

Cora sat erect before me, hands folded in her lap. Any moment now Tom could return from his journey. He could walk through that front door and reenter her life. Any clattering train or smoking bus might bring him back to her.

Or he might never appear again. He might be gone forever. She would not know until it was all over.

"Tom is an alcoholic," she said, as if that explained it all, which it didn't, of course. Alcoholism does not require one to physically leave house and home and wife. What kind of man chooses such a life? I will never get my mind around it.

"I can't understand it," I said.

"Nor can I," she said, and sighed deeply. She turned and looked at a Bible on the table beside her. A shaded lamp, a writing tablet, and a small stack of books were arranged neatly with the Bible closest at hand. "I pray for him every day. I trust that God will take care of him—and me."

I did not ask how she made ends meet on her own, how she maintained her home, or how she paid the bills. The house seemed to be a part of her, mysterious yet revealing, shadows and windows. Through repeated visits I learned to be at ease in Cora's house, though that first morning I was restless and felt out of place. I wanted her husband to be there, I guess, and thought that he might appear suddenly while I was sitting in his chair. I picture him still as a man bent over with the anxieties of life, crippled by his addiction, shuffling down the road dressed in clothes from the local mission. He was pitiful to me, and frightening, too, a symbol of the good and truth that we abandon while chasing longings that cannot satisfy us.

The pain of being rejected and deserted was sometimes in her eyes and voice. She seldom spoke of her husband again, but when she did she would look away from me, staring out a window or fixing on a door as if he might appear. She did not condemn him. She did not communicate any bitterness to me. She had endured his selfish lifestyle. She had chosen to remain with him despite frequent absences that culminated finally in total abandonment.

Cora never saw her husband again as far as I know. He never returned. I preached her funeral, and he was not present.

Cora was married to God, in a way, like a nun. She devoted herself to prayer and to the ministry of the Word. She had become friend and mentor to dozens of people, mostly women, through her years of teaching. Many people found their way to faith in Christ through her example and instruction.

She helped me grow in my own faith. She discussed with me the truths that I tried to explain in my Sunday messages.

Cora knew the Bible front to back. She had a particular eschatology, dispensational and millennial. She expected the end of the world soon. Maybe that expectation emerged from the text of Scripture. Maybe it expressed the longing of her heart to be in a place of peace, without pain.

One day she gave me a book she had ordered for me, hardback and oversized, *The Greatest Book on Dispensational Truth in the World*, authored by a man named Clarence Larkin. I have it still in my library but rarely reference it. It is full of charts and graphs and cartoon-looking figures sketched in black and white, intended to represent the strange beasts and visions of the Book of Revelation. It describes a possible timetable for the end of the world including the rapture of the church and the Great Tribulation.

Cora had specialized in her Bible study. She had focused on prophecy, the Books of Daniel, Ezekiel, and Revelation. She wanted me to know her focus, to understand her perspective. I understood it well. I had learned that view of prophecy as a boy from my father.

We are comforted as Christians by the promises of the Second Coming of Christ, the gathering of the church to heaven, and the victory of the Lamb of God over all evil and pain. We find these truths especially relevant when life is difficult and our hearts are breaking.

Cora could have turned to a different path early in her troubled marriage. She could have stepped out on the husband who cared so little for her. She could have become a wanderer herself, cut loose from her own spiritual moorings by the disappointments and loneliness. Instead she deepened her focus upon God and His Word. She reached out to others who needed encouragement and faith. She became a pillar of strength to all who knew her.

Now you know why I did not want to lose her, my friend and mentor. I was anxious by her bedside in that ICU ward. I did not know that my worries were showing. I have since learned that every emotion I experience is clearly visible in my countenance to those who really know me. My face is a window to my soul.

The ICU staff was bustling around us as I held Cora's hand. I said to her, "Cora, I am going to pray for you." That is one thing you can do whether in a room or a hallway or wherever you are, and you only need a minute or two to open that window to heaven, so I squeezed her hand as she lay on that gurney and prepared to pray.

"You look tired today, Pastor," she whispered suddenly before I began to pray. I opened my eyes and looked at her.

She forced a smile to her lips and said, "Let me pray for you."

I swallowed hard, nodded my head, and closed my eyes, gripping her hand. And Cora prayed for me in the ICU that day, afflicted with the heart problem that would take her life in just a few days. Literally from her deathbed, Cora prayed for me. I do not remember the words. I was moved beyond the words. I was caught up in the thing itself, the inner strength of a woman who, knowing her own peril, insisted on focusing her prayer upon me and my need.

I saw in her a response to suffering and pain that challenged me and changed me. I learned from her that people who truly follow Jesus learn to care for others even when they themselves are hurting. I learned that suffering, difficult as it may be, does not necessarily capture the soul and collapse a life upon itself.

Cora suffered terribly in her life, more than I can imagine or describe, but she did not descend into the darkness of a pain-centered life. She broke free from the prison of pain and reached out to others in their need. In so doing she found solace for her own soul and new purpose in the midst of dreams that died.

Jesus Himself modeled such a response to pain throughout His life and especially as He died upon the Cross. This is why the writer of the Book of Hebrews turned the attention of his fellow sufferers to Jesus:

> *Therefore, since we are surrounded by such a great cloud of witnesses, let us throw off everything that hinders and the sin that so easily entangles. And let us run with perseverance the race marked out for us, fixing our eyes on Jesus, the pioneer and perfecter of faith. For the joy set before him he endured the cross, scorning its shame, and sat down at the right hand of the throne of God. Consider him who endured such opposition from sinners, so that you will not grow weary and lose heart* (Hebrews 12:1–3).

We who seek to follow Jesus in dealing with our pain should fix our eyes upon Him at Calvary, as He died. At the Cross we find truth and strength in our own suffering.

The scene at the Cross is not easy to visit, but imagine it for a moment. Jesus of Nazareth has been suspended between heaven and earth, nailed to a wooden cross. He hangs beside the roadway just outside the city gates of Jerusalem with two other men on crosses, one on each side. His death is approaching. The pain from His wounds is excruciating.

Jesus is suffering both physically and emotionally. The Father in heaven who has always been so close to Him now seems far away. His closest friends have fled. His mother is weeping at the foot of the Cross. People passing by on the road are ridiculing Him. "What a joke," they say, spitting out the words, "a supposed Messiah who cannot even save Himself."

Jesus responded to pain by taking care of other people in His last minutes of life. He thought of the need of his mother, a widow, and asked His Apostle John to care for her. He thought of the thief who was repentant and promised him peace in paradise. He looked at those who had crucified Him and asked God to forgive them.

Caring for others even when you are hurting—that is how the followers of Jesus should respond to pain. That response is faithful to our Lord.

That is what Cora did when she prayed for me on her deathbed, and I have never forgotten it.

Cora straightened her back and refused to allow the pain of her life to defeat her. She walked with a quick step right up to her final hospital visit. Her eyes flashed with determination, and her jaw was set. She had made the decision to commit her life to serving Christ and others, and the suffering she experienced every day could not deter her.

She was following the Lord Jesus as she pressed forward with determination. Those who need encouragement to endure suffering and remain faithful need only look to the Cross of Christ. Here we see the Savior, resolute and unwavering, obedient to the Father until He could say, "It is finished" (John 19:30). I expect the Apostle Paul, beaten and imprisoned himself, was thinking of Jesus when he wrote, "I have finished my course, I have kept the faith" (2 Timothy 4:7 KJV).

The writer of Hebrews used the noun "faith" or the verb "believe" (*pistis* and *pisteuo* in Greek) to describe Christians in their secure relationship to God. Sometimes faith and perseverance seem almost interchangeable in Hebrews: "You need to persevere so that when you have done the will of God, you will receive what he has promised" (Hebrews 10:36); and, "We do not belong to those who shrink back and are destroyed, but to those who have faith and are saved" (Hebrews 10:39).

Suffering certainly tests our faith. The test is often more severe than we ever imagined it would be. When we feel disoriented in our pain, like we are losing our way, we should focus on Jesus Himself, considering His behavior in the midst of His own terrible pain. The faithfulness of Christ will draw us away from bitterness and self-pity that only deepen the darkness. Caring for others even when we are in pain is like turning on the light in a dark room. Suddenly things come back into focus and we realize again the continuing, loving presence of God and our own purpose of love in the world.

FROZEN IN REJECTION

I must tell you that I knocked on her door reluctantly. This was her idea, not mine, and her entire invitation was couched in indecipherable code.

I was busy with important pastoral duties, pushing sticky notes around my desk and throwing away junk mail. The call came in. The assistant buzzed me. I punched the blinking button, picked up the phone, and a strange voice led with stranger words: "I know what you're trying to do, but you can't help, not until you talk to me." Her words dragged me out of my comfortable office.

The situation came uninvited, like having bags of garbage delivered to your door. I knew I was in over my head after the first meeting with George. He told me this meandering tale of marital woe, providing too much unnecessary sexual detail, trying to shock me, I thought. I had decided to abandon any effort at follow-up when his wife, Pam, called. She was a tiny and feisty woman, always at church, and she lit into me with neither sympathy nor restraint. I held that telephone to my ear thinking, *All I did was to listen to his confession, and I am the guilty one?*

Nothing George or Pam had said gave me any inkling of what was behind that third person's door. Trudging up to her porch, I noticed her automobile parked under a weathered carport. It was a classic model, at least 20 years old, with a shiny, bulky bumper and fins on the fenders, faded blue.

The woman who answered the door was tall with blonde hair in a bun on the very top of her head, highlights in gray.

"Pastor Crosby, thank you for coming," she said slowly and deliberately and stepped back to let me in. "Please have a seat." A small couch, fabric worn thin, was the only place to sit. I took one end, she took the other.

A poster framed on the living room wall announced a Las Vegas show coming to the Grand. "My name is Bonnie," she said, and followed my eyes to that poster. "George and I went together to see that show." The date on the poster was more than a decade earlier.

"You must understand, Pastor. He's coming back to me, George is, if his wife will stop threatening him." And so began the decade-old story of a fling with George who swept her off her feet and carried her to Las Vegas. They were perfect for each other, a match made in heaven, Bonnie said, and she was devastated when he went back to his wife upon their return home. She had memorialized their brief time together in every conceivable way. She still fixed her hair just the way George loved it. Her shoes and clothes were what she wore back then. She had not replaced her automobile or changed a single thing about her house. Her life was frozen in time, waiting for his return.

Her affair with George, brief though it may have been, was the central event in her life and in his, she said. Love like that comes only once. One day, she insisted, George would come to his senses and be back at her side.

Bonnie married when she was young. She had divorced years ago. She had no children. She delivered a torrent of words, passionate and fervent, like a pent-up flood. I listened and nodded and occasionally asked a question.

When I said good-bye and stepped outside an hour later, I felt just a little disoriented, like I had fallen into a worm hole or passed through a time warp. When I heard her close the door behind me, I turned and took another look at her small home. The siding and trim needed painting. The shingles were broken and faded. The curtains needed to be replaced. The porch furniture was worn and outdated. The automobile, though, I had to admit, was worth hanging on to.

This woman was making a huge mistake, I felt, as I departed her home. Bonnie was responding to grief and rejection with denial. She was not facing the facts. She was out of touch if not out of her mind, clinging to the hairstyle and clothing that George preferred.

She was right in a way. I could not help George and Pam without knowing the depth of their marital strife and infidelity. But she was also wrong. She saw herself as a current player, involved today with George, when it had been a decade since he even acknowledged her existence. Life was slipping away— ten years already. She had not tried to start over or attempted any new initiative. She was deluded, waiting for an invitation that would never come.

I drove back to the church office mulling over the stalled and twisted relationships in this unholy triangle. I suspected that Bonnie's call to me was not an effort to help but an effort to get back in the game. Anything to feel alive again, I guessed.

George and Pam continued their feud until things exploded once more. He left her and filed for divorce. Instead of reconnecting with Bonnie, George found a new lover. That's when Bonnie called me again. "I have got to talk to you," she said. I could hear the tears in her voice. This time Bonnie was broken, an emotional wreck. I could not console her. Nothing could. The fantasy in which she lived for so many years was over and done. She was overcome with sorrow.

I was afraid at first that Bonnie was suicidal. She was a flood of tears. She went through a box of tissues, but before I left her home that day, I felt her heart turning toward the future. She was beginning to think about the next thing in her life rather than the last thing. The terrible shock of a second rejection woke her up to the rest of her life.

I tell myself and others, "There are no dead ends in God's grace." I believe it. God is full of wisdom and strength. He can provide a new path for me when my old life goes up in flames.

You may be inclined to doubt God in this matter, to believe and insist that life cannot be other than you envisioned it before your dreams collapsed. Pain and grief may have stopped you in your tracks. Maybe you feel debilitated, unable to find a way forward. You should take time to recover from the emotional trauma of rejection and sorrow. No need to rush ahead when you are disoriented and confused. But you should also turn toward your new future in a timely fashion. Your family members and friends—people who love you—are wishing and waiting for your recovery from this blow. They may be praying for you to see your life in a new way.

We do not realize and embrace the fullness of God's grace for ourselves. He is the God of new beginnings! The resurrection of Jesus is proof positive that God can bring joy out of the ashes of any life.

Bonnie stayed too long stuck in denial and delusion, but she eventually faced the truth of her rejection and loss. The last I knew of her, she developed new relationships, new connections and interests in her life. She had moved on from the paralysis of her pain.

Pain has the potential to narrow life down to a tiny point, a single interest or event. When we back away we realize that life is broader and deeper than our single point of pain. Through God's mercy and the power of forgiveness, we can learn to live again and love again even in the wake of our greatest suffering.

SURVIVORS

Survivors was scrawled on a weathered sheet of plywood with a big arrow pointing south toward our church. People who failed to evacuate for Hurricane Katrina must have found it floating on the flood along with a can of dark paint. I saw the sign as I was driving on I-610 near the church just after the breeches in the broken levees had been repaired.

A system of canals captures every drop of water that falls in New Orleans. The drops of water make their way to massive pumping stations that spew them into Lake Pontchartrain. I was packing my daughter's belongings to the street, creating one of those levees of debris, when I noticed that the water level was dropping dramatically. I drove through water to get to her house, but then I saw the crown of the street emerge and then a rivulet in the gutter. I stood over a storm drain as the last drop disappeared off that part of Cortez Street.

The water moves quickly when the pumps are running. The *Survivors* sign was hung on the highway sign when the water was about ten feet deep, I estimated, looking up at it through the windshield. The arrow could have been pointing to our church facility where dozens of people found refuge in the days after the storm. Some of them wrote their names and telephone numbers on our chalkboards. One left a note for me in my office, having slept on the couch.

When you make it alive through a disaster, no matter how battered, you are dubbed a "survivor." Being a survivor may be the loftiest goal to which you can aspire at some moments in your life, depending on the nature of your trouble. Although survival is not the ultimate quest for a person of faith, sometimes it is the closest we can come to the ideal of love. Surviving means I love myself and others enough to keep moving through the pain.

A man who has endured great suffering told me, "I just have to get up in the morning and put one foot in front of the other." That is what survivors do. They walk through the minefields one step at a time. Survivors are not so much interested in the strength to make a journey, just the strength for the next step.

"Boudreaux saw his shadow," a local weatherman said on that first Groundhog Day after Hurricane Katrina. Boudreaux is a nutria. You might think it looks like a really, really large rat, and it is a rodent. Down here in the Bayou Country, the nutria, not the groundhog, sees his shadow. It doesn't have to make sense.

That first Groundhog Day after Katrina was clear and sunny, so we were preparing for an extension of what already seemed like an interminable winter. Beautiful New Orleans became stark and brown prematurely. The greenery was peeled off the earth when Katrina came through on August 29, 2005. The trees were stripped by the winds, and the shrubs and grasses drowned in saltwater.

I was hoping in that following February of 2006 for an early and abundant spring with live oaks clothed in bright new leaves, azaleas and crape myrtles bowing under weighty blooms, and a garment of flowers covering our wounds. Maybe Boudreaux's prediction would prove false.

The chill of that long winter in New Orleans had more to do with dashed hopes than cool temperatures. We felt the cold shoulder of government leaders who had yet to comprehend our plight. We experienced the frosty reception of our plans. A blanket of snowy intentions failed to hide our ruins or warm our hearts. We were frozen in a blizzard of empty promises and useless accusations. The ice was creeping into our souls. The city we loved was in the grip of a frigid winter.

Winter can be beautiful, but that storm-induced winter had been cruel. Five months post-Katrina, a drive through the flood zone would smother your spirits. New Orleans was fully exposed to the elements, ripped open to its core, trapped in mounds of debris, struggling to breathe. Our world was still upside down. Houses remained on top of cars, cars remained on top of fences, billboards hung bottom side up, and household goods hung suspended in trees.

The brown brine line moved across the field of vision like a defect on the screen. That line marked the sustained elevation of the flood. Floating solid and liquid debris created a stain an inch wide and stretching from post to post and house to house for miles. It was often ten feet or more above the street. Even the hardened veterans caught themselves in disbelief, shaking their heads at the evidence, unable to imagine their world under water.

That Groundhog Day I paused in front of Franklin Avenue Baptist Church and observed the stripes across brick and wood and glass. A friend pointed out that the highest water line on the front doors was on the inside of the glass, not the outside. I examined the glass in the entranceway and confirmed my friend's observation. The water line on the inside was about six feet off the floor, eight inches above the highest water line on the exterior. The entire campus was simply part of Lake Pontchartrain for those weeks. Why did the water leave a higher mark inside the glass?

I don't know how that can be. But I know that what happened to the church door happened to me. Inside me, the flood rose even higher, fed by fear and doubt.

Every howling winter, however long, finally gives way to spring. If we fight that claustrophobic cabin fever, we will eventually see blossoms, hear the songs of birds, and enjoy a stroll along the lake. Even if delayed, we will surely see a spring that ends the paralysis and surpasses expectations in its light and its glory.

God sent us such a spring. Long before humans could clean up the mess, God woke up the seeds, sent their shoots pressing toward the sun, and opened their blooms. Piles of debris were decorated with the colors of spring that first year. They were evidence of God's promise, made after the flood, to Noah and me and to all: "As long as the earth endures, seedtime and harvest, cold and heat, summer and winter, day and night will never cease" (Genesis 8:22).

Quell Jenkins trusted in Christ as Savior. She wanted to be baptized. Men in our church carried her up the steps in a chair. They carried her into the water, still on that chair. And one of our ministers baptized her in the pool while she sat in that chair.

Quell was 17 years old when a would-be boyfriend attacked her. He shot her three times and thought he had killed her. She survived, but one bullet damaged her spine. She is a pillar of strength to us, a young woman with faith, joy, and ambition.

The sun will come up in the morning, no matter how difficult the day has been. You might as well get up too.

PILES OF DEBRIS

Picture your home in ten feet of water for three weeks. What do you think would happen?

Imagine peeling off every surface of your house—floor, walls, and ceiling. Imagine throwing away every single stick of furniture—wood, plastic, and metal. Imagine carting all appliances to the street for disposal—refrigerators, stoves, freezers, washers, dryers, icemakers, and trash compactors. New Orleans sported fields of "white debris," the purgatory for all appliances between the home they left and the recycling plant to which they were doomed.

Clothes and food were ruined, as were the vehicle in the garage, the lawn mower in the shed, the pool in the backyard, the fences on the perimeter, the shingles on the roof, the insulation in walls and ceiling, and everything else that you can imagine. Even pots and pans, dishes and plates, and silverware were marred and discarded. People came with rental trucks to take their salvageable possessions back to their new homes somewhere else. They left with empty trucks and, maybe, one small garbage can of tarnished memorabilia.

The levees of debris grew until they stretched from one intersection to another. The debris crept past the curb and into the street. The trucks beat the plasterboard into a fine dust that settled on every surface. Its acrid odor filled the air. Breathing was inadvisable if a vehicle passed. Jogging for morning exercise was no longer advisable either.

The stench of the city rose up toward heaven—hundreds of thousands of freezers full of ruined meat. No resident of New Orleans will forget that awful smell that lingered in the air for weeks and hung on the nostrils. Foolish newcomers moved the freezers and refrigerators without taping them like they were living organisms trying to escape. Only when fully bound and impossible to open were they really safe to move.

"Patient in tribulation" became a favorite verse of mine (Romans 12:12 KJV). Everything moved slower than anyone could justify. Traffic lights did not function. Residential streets were a single lane between mounds of refuse.

The street I live on is named Marseilles Street. Hurricane Katrina broke the street sign in half. I lived on "Mars" for months. It truly felt like a strange planet everywhere I went. A trip outside the flood zone was like a drink of pure water from the well, a refreshing blast of fresh air. I didn't know how oppressed I was by my circumstances until I found a temporary reprieve.

Love This City has been the theme of First Baptist New Orleans since 1996. Many people have asked me what exactly that phrase means—*love this city*. Some have even left the church because they felt that they did not and could not *love this city*.

Loving this city is all about loving its people. Interpreted in this way, Jesus' followers really have no choice. We are called to love our neighbors like we love ourselves. Undoubtedly, that is difficult work. It may even be impossible. Nevertheless, the teaching of Jesus is clear. He insists that we love our neighbor, love our enemies, and even love those who hurt us and persecute us. Reading Jesus, you would think that love is the answer to every human question!

A young couple in our church finally tied the knot. They postponed their wedding twice because of Katrina and her aftermath. They remained in good spirits; "Love is patient," as the Apostle Paul so eloquently declared in 1 Corinthians 13:4.

I ran into a family that moved back months after evacuating to North Carolina when Katrina approached. Their home flooded, of course, and they were living in a hotel while enduring the endless wait for a FEMA trailer. She was a teacher in Orleans Parish public schools for many years and was subsequently unemployed, obviously. They worked on their home until the last sunlight faded day after day, they told me after our hugs and greetings. Then they rushed to the grocery store to secure chicken for supper—the one thing they wanted after a hard day of cleaning up the mess. The meat department ran out of chicken just before they arrived.

They had no home, but they had friends.

They had no travel trailer, but they had hope.

She had no job, but he had his, and they were grateful.

Her school was closed, but her son's school, Brother Martin, was open.

They had no chicken for supper, but they found something else to eat, and it was fine.

Love is patient.

Love is not passive. Love is not inactive. Love is not a doormat. But love is patient.

People who love New Orleans have always had to be patient with her, especially post-Katrina, and that meant being patient with neighbors and grocers and out-of-state drivers and leaders who sometimes floundered and foundered.

Patience is not burying your head in the sand. Patience is the resolve to remain in a situation even though it is difficult and painful. Patience is the strength to continue to work for change even when the progress is slow. Patience is persistence in the struggle. It is consistency when planning is impossible. It is courage on a daily basis.

And patience is absolutely necessary when trouble comes.

Our church facility was in the flood zone of New Orleans. We were told in October that it would be sometime in May before we had telephone service (it was actually July). When I heard this, I wanted to tear out what little hair I had left. I wanted to throttle somebody.

Frustration ran high among the ruins of our city. Inconvenience was part of our lives. Nothing was as easy as it used to be. Patience came to our rescue. Without it we would have been twisted in knots, thrashing inside our creeping vehicles, fuming in long lines, and shouting at the people who could not help us and were as frustrated as we.

Patience is the companion of faith and hope. Patience receives this day, with all of its challenges, as a gift of grace. Patience corrects our vision, puts life back into perspective, and allows us to enjoy the good things about this moment.

Patience is essential for any craftsman who is building a superior product. It is vital for every artist who is seeking to excel. It is the friend and facilitator of our finest future.

We could not see it then, but we were living in a world of giants. Composers and poets and painters would memorialize the travails of our march from the ruins. Our words and deeds would be translated into song and verse and woven into the fabric of history and culture for future generations. For good or ill, the great task of rebuilding fell to us, and it became our challenge and privilege to overcome through patient endurance.

I have changed my opinion. When first the flood came, I felt that we had fallen under the judgment of God. Now I see that we are the objects of His special favor. He chose us to help restore the jewel of the South, called by many the apple of His eye, the most interesting city in America.

Be patient, friends in tribulation. God is accomplishing His work in you.

UNEXPECTED EMBRACE

Three of the women are dead. Thinking of it now startles me.

I watched as they popped a cassette tape into a plastic player sitting on the bare concrete floor. The music began, vocal and instrumental, tinny through the small speaker, and the quartet of ladies signed the words in flowing motions, beautifully choreographed, in perfect synchronization, expressing the love and the goodness of God.

Their white uniforms seemed more like costumes then, and matched the smiles on their faces. Were they all sincere in their faith, I wondered, or was some of this "jailhouse religion"? I knew three of the four quite well, having spent two hours weekly with them for six years.

"I think she is genuine," Bill insisted later, gripping his coffee cup with one hand and rapping his knuckles in the air with the other. The prison and its infamous inmates were often the talk over coffee in Gatesville. "Emily watches her five days a week, walking that pipe chase. She lives it just like she talks it."

The pipe chase he spoke of was a corridor of metal pipes and mesh along which prison guards walked in the maximum security Mountainview Unit for women. Bill's wife, Emily, worked the pipe chase on death row. Four women were incarcerated there at that time, including Karla Faye Tucker, their most renowned prisoner. The brutality of her homicides made front-page news in Houston, as did her trial and the death penalty the jury handed down. Karla was the first woman executed in Texas in 135 years.

The first time I saw Karla she barely spoke. I had no idea who she was or what she might have done. She was in the second row of cells at the far end of the psychiatric ward. That is where death row was located when I first began a weekly Bible study with those inmates condemned to die. I walked in the middle of that concrete corridor on my trips to death row, trying to stay beyond the reach of mentally ill prisoners on either side. If they chose to throw urine or excrement, though, I could not avoid it. They were always loud and often vulgar.

Perhaps that accounted for Karla's silence for the first weeks of her stay at Mountainview. That location had to be the worst in all of the Texas Department of Criminal Justice. Sometimes we could not hear ourselves talk or sing or even think above the protests and screams of the criminally insane.

Karla "fell" in Houston, as the prison lingo goes. She committed her crime, was arrested, charged, and convicted there.

She also found salvation through Christ in the Houston jail. A chaplain told Karla, the cold-blooded killer, about the love of God received through Jesus. Karla, the daughter of a prostitute and drug addict, had followed in her mother's footsteps and developed a penchant for violence. She had never heard the good news about God's forgiveness that every person needs to hear. She had lived in a deep, dark hole all her life.

As soon as the good news reached her, Karla received it with joy. She was transported after her conviction in a "chain" of women from the Harris County Jail to the maximum security unit for women. She came to death row in Gatesville, Texas, as a brand-new believer, not really knowing anything about the Bible or how to walk with Christ.

She soon began to ask questions and participate in the discussion. I would sit on the concrete floor in the corridor that hit its end at death row. The women would crowd up to the metal bars. I talked and sang there for an hour or two each Monday. Pam Perillo was in the last cell on the right when I began the Bible study. Eventually her death sentence was commuted to life in prison, but she stayed on death row for many years.

Betty Beats joined us some time later, then Frances Newton. Death row was moved to a much better setting after a couple of years, a cell block away from the other prisoners. That's where the quartet did their signing. That's where I had Thanksgiving one year.

That's where I learned that Karla continually expressed sorrow for her crimes, which she acknowledged. She received God's forgiveness for her sins. She was at peace in that regard. But the families of her victims had spoken during the sentencing phase. They were wounded, bereaved, traumatized, and angry, as anyone would be who lost a loved one to a drug-crazed psychopath wielding a pickax.

Peggy Kurtz, sister to Karla's victim Jerry Dean, sent Karla a note and told her that she forgave her. She asked Karla to call if that was ever a possibility. Eventually Karla and Peggy had a telephone conversation. Karla expressed to her how sorry she was for her crime, and Peggy responded by telling Karla, "I forgive you."

Much of our sorrow and pain is caused by the sinful choices of other people. That is true for all of us. God calls us to forgive those who have hurt us. We are to forgive others as the Father in heaven has forgiven us. This forgiveness may or may not bless the one who committed the sin, but without doubt it blesses the life of the one who does the forgiving. We send away our sorrow and our pain by forgiving those who hurt us. Until we forgive, we are harboring and nurturing the resentment and the bitterness that do great damage to our inner life and our relationships.

The women on death row all learned sign language when Betty Beats, one of their number, went deaf. Karla initiated the lessons. This exercise in compassion and mutual understanding is symbolic to me of the spiritual transformation that Karla experienced through the love and forgiveness of Christ.

We are called to forgive others not only for their slight injuries and minor offenses against us. We are called to forgive those who perpetrate major crimes upon us and our loved ones. We must forgive them too. There is no prison on earth more formidable than that of an unforgiving heart.

Years later another family member of one of Karla's victims had the rare opportunity to talk to her face-to-face. In that encounter, those present witnessed the surprising embrace between a murderer and a brother she left bereaved.

Victims of crimes are often ignored. They suffer the loss of property and relationships. They suffer the indignities of poverty and destitution as a result of crimes committed against them. I have told you about Quell who was paralyzed for life after being shot by an angry high school classmate. Her life was forever changed.

Victims of crime must work to forgive just like the rest of us. We suffer through all kinds of hurt and heartache—abandonment, divorce, violence, and criminal negligence. We recover from our injuries in part by learning to forgive. No need for us to be hindered and hampered all our lives by anger and resentment. We all want to get to joy, peace, and love. Forgiveness is the way there. For the sake of those we love, we've got to let go of the anger.

God does not suggest that we extend forgiveness for some cases but not for others. His instructions are clear: "Bear with each other and forgive one another if any of you has a grievance against someone. Forgive as the Lord forgave you" (Colossians 3:13). God's forgiveness blankets our life from west to east and north to south, from our first breath to our last. We are completely forgiven, washed white as snow inside, through the work of Christ upon the Cross.

This amazing, wall-to-wall forgiveness from God is the model for our own forgiveness. No use us trying to hang on to the big offenses, forgiving only those who deserve it. We did not and do not deserve the forgiveness of God. Forgiving those who do not deserve to be forgiven is the core of God's forgiveness plan.

Karla got just such unmerited forgiveness, first from God and then from Peggy. Peggy followed God in her path to forgiveness. She forgave her brother's killer because she felt compelled by the forgiveness of Christ to do so.

Let it go. Give it up. Open up your heart and roll out all the anger and bitterness that resides within. Forgive those who have hurt you. It's the way that Jesus showed us, and He did say, "Follow me."

PUNCH A HOLE IN THAT VOLCANO

"I'm going to Peru," I told the men at Mona's Coffee.

"Now what are you going to do in Peru?" one of them asked.

"We are collecting eyeglasses, thousands of them. I am taking an optometrist, and we are going to give these old glasses to people in the mountains who have vision problems." I never dreamed how emotional I would become when I saw elderly followers of Jesus weeping as they read their Bibles, enabled by those glasses. Handcrafts, too, were essential to their well-being. The eyeglasses proved to be an amazing gift, so practical for so many.

Mountain villagers in the northern part of Peru insisted that we join in a feast one day. They caught a guinea pig or two, dressed them up, and mixed the meat into the rice. The sun had dipped below the mountaintops by the time I made it to dinner. A single lightbulb suspended from a wire a dozen feet from the door failed to illuminate the room. I could see the food was arranged on the floor. Later I learned that the utensils had all been washed in the stream a few steps from the house.

I got so sick that night. By the time we made the trip back to the home where I was staying, my stomach was thrashing like a million bugs were fighting one another. A wise physician had given me a bottle of pills to pack in my suitcase. "Take one of these," he said, "when you know you are getting sick." I rushed to my room, scrambled through my stuff, found that bottle, and swallowed one of those pills. It felt like a silent explosion in my stomach, that pill hitting those bugs. The storm in my stomach subsided, and all the bugs died.

My ailment was familiar to the Quechua Indians who live in the northern reaches of the Andes Mountains. Their infant mortality rate was 60 percent, a staggering figure that cannot begin to communicate the sorrow of bereaved mothers and fathers. Ninety percent of those infants were dying because of the polluted water in their streams and rivers. They had no magic pills to stop the dysentery that took the lives of their babies and made them all so sick.

Larry and Joy made a difference in that infant mortality rate. They were simple people, ranchers from Texas, married for decades. At 50 years of age, they sensed God calling them to be missionaries. They sold the ranches and moved to Peru.

"Do you have any regrets?" I asked Larry late one night. We had stopped the old Range Rover on top of a mountain pass, turned off the engine, and were enjoying the star-studded sky with not a single artificial light competing—like Inca warriors saw it long ago. The tired engine was clicking and hissing its way to cool. The heat of the hood felt good against my forearms.

"Only one," he said as he turned toward me. "I wish I had done it sooner."

Abundant life happens in the arc of relationship between two people. That relationship delivers maximum spiritual satisfaction when one life is laid down on behalf of the other. The person most rewarded in this act of life-giving is the one who gives rather than the one who receives. When such giving alleviates extreme human suffering, the rewards on both sides are transformational.

I climbed into the passenger seat of that battered Range Rover early one morning and rode with Larry on rough mountain lanes to a remote village 10,000 feet above sea level. The clinic would open in a couple of hours. We needed to be ready for hundreds of people. A team of oxen was pulling a plow through a field with a young man walking behind them.

"Larry, what are they growing?" I asked.

"A new variety of corn or wheat that we have introduced for these high altitudes," he said. Then he gestured toward a cone-shaped mountain east of us. "We irrigate this land from a lake in that volcano," he said. "We punched a hole in the side of the mountain and pipe the water to these fields."

I stared at the rocky peak as the oxen made their rounds. I was thinking to myself, *If we have the will, God will make a way for us to help people in need.* Many of the things that cause terrible suffering in the world—disease, war, much of the lack of food and drinkable water—could be prevented or cured if people who have the resources and know how to do things would find their way to those who don't. I expect that one day God may ask us about our efforts to help the widows and the orphans in our world—and the millions who do not have enough to eat and suffer from easily preventable diseases.

Larry drilled 33 wells in northern Peru. Every well was soon surrounded by a community that developed along the water lines. No one wants their children to get sick and die. When people around Cajamarca learned that safe water was available, they found a way to access that water.

We who lived through Hurricane Katrina will never forget the many people who came to our rescue in the wake of that great storm. Followers of Jesus were especially prominent among those who came to help. It was a powerful witness to the love of God and an appropriate response to the suffering of many in this region.

Most everyone agrees, whatever their religious persuasion, that alleviating suffering is a good thing to do. We should not harm our neighbors—we should help them. Whether delivering a cup of cold water or poking a hole in a volcano, followers of Jesus should be busy helping the hurting, feeding the hungry, and addressing human need wherever they find it.

EMBRACE THE FUTURE

I grew up on the road. My family was huge, but we all rode together in the car or truck. We loved to travel together. Those trips were the best of times to me. I kept my nose pressed against the window, watching the world go by.

Dad was not a planner. We joke among ourselves about it. He built a house on the prairie north of Gatesville. I was there when the work started. We lifted the 12-foot-long 2-by-8 pine boards out of the tall grasses, nailed them together, and made 6 grids with cross members on 24-inch centers. Then we leveled the first grid on cinder blocks set in the grass where Mom and Dad decided. When all 6 grids were perfectly level, we nailed them together. That is how we began. No charts. No drawings that I can remember. No footers or piers.

"You know how Crosbys take a vacation?" one in-law asked me.

"No. How?" I responded, already chuckling.

"You load the car, drive to the end of the driveway, then ask the family, 'Which way do you want to turn?'"

Maybe it was not that spontaneous, growing up with Russell (Dad) at the wheel, but sometimes it got close.

Those trips were so interesting to me. My favorite seat was by the window. When Dad said, "Get in!" I ran to the car, grabbed the armrest on the door, hung on tightly, and swung with it until the car was loaded. The only person who gets fresh air in a car with that many passengers is the person by the window. Even more important, it's the best view.

I learned as a boy that I could only concentrate on a feature in the landscape for a few seconds. If something intriguing appeared on the horizon, I would watch it grow, study it as it drew near, and get the best look I could as we passed by. But I could not study it or watch it any longer once it was behind us. It faded away into the distance. And if I didn't pay attention to what was coming, I would miss the interesting scenes ahead.

Life is like that. You have to let go of the past, good or bad. You cannot change it, and you cannot live there. "All that life is dead," the songwriter said of the past ("Vincent," Don McLean), and in a way it is.

Our God is the God of the future as well as of the present and the past. He knows the future. He will bring world history to its proper conclusion in Christ. We are people who trust in a good God who does all things well.

God saved us by His grace at great cost. He could have transported us to heaven to be with Him at that very moment of our spiritual rescue. Instead, He left us here in a world full of hurt and trouble. He asks us to join Him in spreading words and deeds of love. We are God's partners in this good work. One day all of God's people will be in a place with no sorrow or suffering, but for right now, we are commissioned to go tell the good news of forgiveness and to love our neighbor as God has loved us. Both our words and our deeds are aimed at human suffering.

Embrace the future. Don't fear it. Don't turn from it. Embrace it. It is coming at you no matter what you do. Expect it to be good. Prepare to be a blessing to those around you.

Every follower of Jesus needs to learn to pray something like this: *God of the future, help me to receive what is coming my way with grace and faith and great expectation. Use me to craft a better future for those I love.*

ACCIDENT AND INJURY

I first learned of Graham's accident from my oldest child, Rachel, who was living in Mississippi. It was a brief call: "Graham fell into a bucket of water. Rebekah said he is not breathing. I am packing to go to New Orleans now. I don't know anything else."

I sat still for a moment when she hung up, cell phone in hand, listening to dead airspace. I put down the phone slowly and looked through the window toward the Reagan Building across the street. I know cars were stopping at the traffic light, but I didn't see them. I know people were using the crosswalk, but I didn't notice.

Graham, my ten-month-old grandson, was not breathing, I told myself, but still it didn't sink in. Graham was the active one, crawling now at champion pace, pulling up and getting into everything. Janet had just moved the coffee table to a corner so Graham would not keep pulling up on it and toppling over on whatever was in the way.

Graham had no fear. He knew nothing about consequences it seemed. He darted behind Nina's back just the other day and lunged off the bed, hitting his tough forehead on the nightstand. I was standing right there and couldn't stop him. He was just too fast.

I wondered where he was when it happened. It was 5:00 p.m. in Washington, D.C., so 4:00 p.m. central time. I felt my throat constrict, realizing the accident might have happened while he was in the care of my wife, Janet, his Nina, who kept him almost every day. I thought about how devastating that would be to her. Graham has a huge presence in our hearts and our home. His toys are assembled by the fireplace. A basket at the end of the loveseat holds his diapers, wipes, powder, and ointments.

His infant seat is anchored in my car, his stroller parked in the living room. His little clothes tumble with ours in the dryer, and his bottles sit in the cupboard.

The possibility of losing Graham was too deep a terror to contemplate. I could not entertain the thought. I had hurt for my father as I watched him slowly die, but I never felt terror through his long journey of heart disease. Learning of Graham's accident precipitated in me a flood of panic and fear.

He is not breathing, I thought, then said it out loud to my friends. I related to them, haltingly, my short conversation with Rachel. They hailed a taxi, made flight arrangements, and took care of all details. I tried to read on the flight home. I went to the tiny restroom and stared at my reflection. I even said the words to myself in the mirror, "He is not breathing." I said them out loud again and again, staring at my reflection. They did not seem real, no matter how I said them.

Pain and sorrow and trouble are disorienting, sometimes shocking. They throw you off your game and off your feet. Often the deepest trouble comes without warning, with no time to prepare. You get the call, and that is it. You cannot rewind. No one can explain it. The universe has changed fundamentally, without your knowledge or permission, and you are left to adjust.

I walked down the concourse of the airport in New Orleans, one foot in front of the other. A friend picked me up and drove me to the hospital. I walked out of the elevator on the fourth floor and stumbled into the embrace of my friends who waited there for me, and the whole disaster became a little more real. Their presence there, six dear friends in front of me, communicated to me what I could not bring myself to accept. Seeing my family members in that hospital room, seeing my daughter weeping, then seeing my little grandson on the ventilator, drew me into a vortex of grief from which I could not escape.

My daughter's suffering in the wake of her son's accident is the deepest sorrow I have witnessed in my life. She told me after that first week of Graham's stay in ICU that she had lost eight pounds. *That's about what a gallon of tears weighs*, I thought to myself. Rebekah wept nonstop for nearly three days. Her weeping became a small pause in conversation, like saying "uh" or "you know." She would comment about, say, the doctor's Texas roots, weep for a little while in the midst of it, and then tell us which town he was from.

Rebekah had a picture in her head, the image of her baby boy upside down in a bucket. She turned away for just a second, washing the car in their driveway, and Graham scrambled around the car, pulled up, and plunged over. The white plastic bucket did not tip over, though it held only three inches of soapy water. Graham was too little to pull himself out.

She held his limp body in her arms. He was not breathing. She laid him in the grass. She screamed for help. She pumped his chest. She pinched his little nose and blew into his mouth. She needed to call 911. But, in her panic, she could not find it. She rushed to her house door, Graham in her arms. The door was locked. She fumbled to punch in the security code. Four times she tried, shaking and frantic, without success.

A neighbor out walking her dog saw Rebekah in her need. She stopped, assessed the situation, and flagged down an older couple. They took Graham from his mother and began to administer CPR (cardiopulmonary resuscitation). The man called 911.

Rebekah finally found her cell phone and called her husband, Michael. He arrived in seconds, and began to try to revive Graham. The older couple again took a turn with CPR. Rebecca, a teenager, walked by. She saw the situation and began to administer infant CPR, as she had learned it in a high school classroom.

The dog was barking. Brady, Graham's three-year-old brother, was crying. People were doing what they could to help both Graham and his parents.

The EMTs (emergency medical technicians) arrived quickly and took over CPR. A fifth mouth pressed against the baby's mouth. They found no pulse. Graham was not breathing. They rushed the baby and Rebekah to the hospital three miles away.

Doctors found a faint pulse only when Graham reached the emergency room 30 minutes after the accident. When I learned this, I sunk like a rock into the sea of despair.

THREE DAYS NEAR THE TOMB

Life unraveled into chaos.

Sitting in the waiting room, I thought of the second verse in the Bible: "The earth was formless and empty, darkness was over the surface of the deep." That just about summed it up for me right then.

The clock in the waiting room was affixed to the wall at eye level. The battery was dead. For some reason I checked it every time I passed. It never moved, of course. I decided to find a battery and get the dead clock ticking, but I forgot about it as soon as something else came up. Minutes and hours passed by silently, but life didn't go anywhere. Everything outside of the little boy in the bed receded into irrelevance. We spent two weeks in that waiting room. The clock did not tick when we got there or when we left.

I first arrived at the hospital around 10:30 p.m., six hours after the accident. Graham was in critical condition. He had been intubated. EMTs had administered emergency IVs by stabbing the shinbones on both legs. He was not breathing on his own, but his heart was beating. His lungs were working minimally.

We endured a long night.

The next morning, maybe 16 hours after the accident, we were notified of a pending consultation with the doctor. We wove our way single file deeper into the ICU, following the quick steps of a social worker, and took our seats in an empty hospital room. Janet and I; grandparents Bill and Sue Deris; husband, Michael Deris; our daughter, Rebekah; and our oldest daughter, Rachel, sat in a circle formed by couches and chairs assembled from different rooms.

The lead physician in the pediatric intensive care unit (PICU) stepped through the door and greeted us. He was tall and thin and matter-of-fact. He sat down on an empty stool in the circle, hooked a heel on the circular bar around its base, and leaned forward with a hand on his knee.

"I am going to be honest with you," the physician said. He looked young to me, draped in that white coat, blue jeans underneath. "This is how I see it: You are facing three possibilities with Graham. First, you need to prepare for the possibility that he may not survive this ordeal. He may die." He paused a moment, and his words fell upon our hearts like a shadow. We sat silent and motionless in our chairs.

"Second, he may survive, but he may sustain serious brain injury." We all had already contemplated this possibility, but hearing it spoken out loud in that moment jolted us. No one asked a question. Maybe no one was breathing.

"Third, he could survive and have no brain injury. That is a possibility." The doctor looked around the circle and then back to Michael and Rebekah. "We don't know how this will go. The first three days are critical."

The injured brain swells to its maximum in those first 72 hours, a nurse explained later. The swelling itself could injure the brain even further or even be fatal for Graham. They would monitor him closely and do everything possible to prevent the swelling.

We began to breathe and eat and try to sleep in this three-day parenthesis of unknown outcomes.

Losing a child must surely be one of the deepest sorrows human beings experience. When you feel that you have contributed to the death of your child, that sorrow is deeper still.

The guilt and shame and sorrow of losing Graham gripped my daughter's heart and would not let go. For three days she suffered agony beyond description. It doubled her up in pain, pulling her into a fetal position. It left her gasping for breath, unable to speak.

My own sorrow over the possible—even probable—loss of Graham was matched by the sorrow I felt for Rebekah. No medicine could touch her pain. Nothing medical science had to offer could reach that deep. She was hurting in a place no one could touch but God.

WISE COMFORTERS DRAPED IN SILENCE

Genuine comforters came to our aid, three young mothers with children who had known Rebekah for many years. Holly and Heather traveled from Texas; Kristen lives here in New Orleans. Holly and Kristen had both suffered the loss of a child; Heather is the mother of four children. These women, among many others, sat with us in the waiting room, fetching water or cleaning the table, venturing only into small talk about normal life, not suggesting any cures or any reasoning. These wise women knew that the pain Rebekah felt could not be soothed by words.

My daughter was not suffering from a lack of understanding. She had an image burned into her brain, a picture of her baby boy blue and lifeless, upside down in a bucket of water. Every time she blinked that image flashed across her eyes, and she caved in again.

Maybe it was this way with Mary and Martha when their dear brother Lazarus died. Maybe they cried until they fell exhausted in the bed. Maybe all their tears were spent when Jesus finally came to them. Maybe all they thought about was the sorrow of those hours just passed. Both of them said, "Lord, if you had been here, my brother would not have died" (John 11:21, 32).

I am confident these sisters had disturbing images in their minds. They cared for their brother through his terminal illness.

They prepared his body for burial. They marched in sorrow to the cemetery and closed up that tomb.

I wonder now if those sisters ever recovered completely from the death of their brother. A miraculous restoration of your loved one does not eliminate three days of sorrow from your mind and heart and soul. They walked through the terror and the tears of those days. They experienced the emotional and spiritual concussion of his death.

The disciples saw Jesus after the Resurrection: "They worshiped him, but some doubted" (Matthew 28:17). The doubt they felt may have been connected to the depth of grief and confusion upon His death. Having suffered three days of despair, their hearts could not rebound immediately. They laid upon the cold stone the beaten and lifeless body of the Promised One. The grave was sealed off, and so too were all their aspirations in this life.

A miracle does not rewind time, I am discovering. Three days pressed near the death of a child makes a deep and lasting impression on your heart. The long and inconsolable grief of losing a child is impossible for me to imagine, especially given our three-day vigil with the prospect of such a loss looming over us.

Rebekah said it in the waiting room in the presence of her wonderful friends. She would not despair of the goodness of God even if her baby died. This type of trust reminds me of Job 13:15: "Though he slay me, yet will I hope in him."

I felt that way, too, though I did not say it out loud at the time. I have been with grieving parents many times. I have walked that valley with them as best I could. I have seen the sorrow that crushes the soul, the faces wet with tears and bodies racked with pain. The tragedy involving my own grandson, though, was not a journey of empathy or pastoral ministry. It was my personal assignment, inexplicably and unexpectedly thrust upon me. I never questioned the goodness of God in that journey, but I did feel the unsettling and sobering presence of sorrow and death in a new way. I experienced one dimension of the future that lies ahead for me and all the people I love.

People who live a long time see lots of death. Sometimes they become stranded in their longevity, outlasting all their friends and family and ending up alone on this earth. I experienced in Graham's hospital room the feeling that life was upside down. *My grandson's death should not precede my own.*

I moderate business meetings and use *Robert's Rules of Order*. Sometimes a member of the group will make a motion that is out of order, and the moderator must rule it as such. It feels like an insult, but it is really only a way of keeping the meeting on point. *God should rule this out of order*, I thought, standing by Graham and listening to the ventilator. *This is wrong, fundamentally wrong.*

The truth is hard to understand and even harder to endure. We all die. Sometimes people die in an order we perceive to be fair and right. Many times they do not. My grief over Graham's possible death seemed to be connected to all that he would miss in life—growing up, loving his family, making his contribution. Then I realized that these were things I would miss, not Graham. If Graham died, he would go to heaven to be with God. He would never have a sense of missing anything down here.

We may perceive the self-centeredness of our grief more clearly when our loved ones are old and infirm and ready to die. Efforts to keep them here with us start to look like cruelty rather than kindness. I have thought, *God waits to take them until we have made the adjustment in our own souls.* As soon as we reconcile ourselves to the truth that they are better off with Him than with us, we may have a sense of peace about their death. God receives them into eternal peace.

Even when our children die, the tears are largely for our own loss. We know this when we think about it. The sorrow we feel is legitimate, right, and true. But the little ones who die have no sorrow at all concerning what they missed. Like the elders who die in Christ, they have perfect peace. In heaven, there are no tears (Revelation 21:4).

I could not endure the thought of life without Graham, standing there by his bedside, but I knew that life would go on for him and for us, even if he died. I assumed that what the Lord spoke to Paul would also be true for us: "My grace is sufficient for you" (2 Corinthians 12:9).

I could not imagine any shortfall in the grace of Christ. Nor could I imagine how I and the family would make it if Graham died. Though I could not see a clear way forward, I had confidence in my heart that God would provide a way through the valley for all of us, including his brokenhearted mother.

Rebekah experienced a grief that seemed life-threatening to me, like her own heart would simply explode if Graham died. At one point she voiced the thought that Graham's death would be hers as well. I began to rehearse the words I might say to her if Graham did not survive: "Brady needs you. Mike needs you. We need you." But all words, no matter how well-intended, seemed limp and futile before the prospect of Graham's death.

I believed that God's grace would be sufficient for us whatever His answer might be. This was my response to God, though feeble in faith, during that three-day interlude between the accident and the announcement by the physician that Graham was past the critical period and would likely survive the ordeal.

I continue to walk in that all-sufficient grace during the longer-term spiritual adjustments that are required by my grandson's brush with death.

We try to push death and dying to the back of our minds. Maybe we have to do so. When a child nearly dies, we relearn the truth that no one is bulletproof. Everybody dies. Death has a renewed presence both intellectually and emotionally. We don't want to be morbid—caught up in the reality of death. Certainly there are other realities, and they are just as true and certain as the grave, but the Bible begins and ends with issues of life and death, and these are never ignored in true faith.

Some may suppose that faith consists in never acknowledging sickness or death. The Bible teaches us otherwise. "Lazarus is dead," Jesus said (John 11:14). Epaphroditus almost died, Paul wrote (Philippians 2:27). These words declare the truth. Truth is the friend of genuine faith, not its enemy.

I come away from the bedside of Graham with a great sense of mystery concerning the mercy of God. Holly lost her baby shortly after birth. Kristen's baby, though full-term, never got to take a breath. These two mothers came to sit silently with Rebekah. Silence is appropriate in the presence of unfathomable mystery.

Job's friends sat in silence with him, not speaking a word, for seven days (Job 2:13). Their silent presence was far more helpful to him in his misery than the subsequent challenges and accusations that proceeded from their mouths. Sometimes we hesitate to be present with those in pain because we "do not know what to say." Not knowing what to say should really be the least of our worries. Our silence in the face of suffering communicates humility, honesty, and genuineness. As we run errands, provide food and drink, clean up the waiting room, or wash the dishes, we are speaking our love without words.

God alone is the arbiter of life and death. Rebekah's friends prayed, too, in the throes of their crises, but they received a different answer. We do not know why or how these things come to pass. We can guess about certain things. We can apply logic and philosophy and theology, but in the end our calculations are not conclusive or exhaustive. We stand silent before the mystery of God's providence.

PEDIATRIC INTENSIVE CARE:
AN EXERCISE IN HELPLESSNESS

Graham survived those first three critical days after nearly drowning. Commonly the brain swells in those first 72 hours, often causing death or brain injury. Blood tests did not indicate injury by oxygen deprivation to his heart, kidneys, liver, or bowels. His lungs were seriously injured from the dirty water, but Rebekah had used an environmentally friendly soap that had no caustic chemicals in it. The doctors were hopeful his lungs would recover. We were in a marathon, not a sprint, we were told.

The carafe must have sat on the warmer through the wee hours of the morning, cooking the coffee. I found a small plastic foam cup in the break room, maybe six ounces, and watched the black brew fill it up. It smelled burned, acrid. A heaping teaspoon of powdered creamer turned it a dark chocolate color instead of khaki. It was 5:00 a.m., and I needed caffeine. I added a packet of sugar, swirled it with a black straw, then drained the cup and tossed it in the trash can.

I stepped across the hall, heard the beeping machines, and checked to see if my grandson was moving. He was still, asleep I guessed, and I was grateful. When the nurses changed his diaper, cleaned him up, suctioned his mouth and his lungs, he fought them all the way. It was exhausting to watch.

I heaved a sigh, walked past his bed, and sat down on a heap of sheets and blankets piled on a lumpy couch turned into a bed. My daughter and son-in-law, completing their all-night vigil, had gone home to shower and have breakfast with a friend. I was in something of a routine, showing up at the PICU around 5:00 a.m. and relieving them for a spell.

The room was dark. The glass wall that separated the hospital room from the hallway was covered by a curtain stretched to full length. A sign on the sliding glass door read, *No stimulation*. Sounds were kept at a minimum. Conversations were confined to whispers.

Sitting down, I was at eye level with the top of the crib. Each of the four sides swiveled on a central pin. The side before me, like the others, was a gray plastic grid with a grip in the center to raise and lower the rail. A larger plastic tube ran from Graham's mouth over the rail on the opposite side and dipped down to the ventilator that hissed and throbbed with regular rhythm day and night.

Graham was a small figure, even in the child's bed. Eight different medications were suspended above his head. Clear plastic tubing curled downward from each dispenser into the port taped securely on the right side of Graham's groin. Computer screens on either side of the bed continuously reported information about body temperature, blood pressure, heart rate, and lung activity. Half a dozen zigzag lines indicated the peaks and valleys of pulmonary performance.

A new screen, installed just for one night, showed the electrical impulses in various parts of the brain. The electrodes—and the top of Graham's head—were covered by a wrapping of white cloth. The EEG (electroencephalogram) drew endless squiggly lines, dozens of them. I could not imagine how anyone could actually "read" such a thing, though I am told they can.

Graham was lying on a special mat designed to lower body temperature and slow down the body's metabolism, decreasing demand for oxygen. The family pediatrician saw this device for the first time at Graham's bedside—the latest in care for drowning victims. It simulated the effects of a fall into ice water. The cool temperature of the body reduces damage and contributes to the long-term health of the organs. Graham's body temperature hovered around 90 degrees.

The medical team did not want Graham to fight the ventilator or the feeding tube. They kept him on painkillers, sedatives, and paralytic drugs to minimize discomfort and let his body heal. The medications were regulated so that the baby stayed just below consciousness, surfacing occasionally to open his eyes.

I suspected the world looked like a big blur to him. It felt like that to me. The last week seemed to lack both length and depth. Time was rationed in short breaths and tiny heartbeats. Good news sent us up like rockets; bad news made us crash like falling rocks. We felt the peaks and valleys but lost the middle.

A nurse pushed aside the closed curtain and entered the room. I stepped up to the railing of Graham's bed. He was crying, but he could make no sound. The intubation interfered with his vocal chords. The morning routine of the shift change began in the PICU.

THE SEIZURES: SETBACK TO GOD KNOWS WHERE

A white-coated technician walked into the room. Graham grimaced, and his mouth opened in a silent wail as she peeled off the electrodes on his head. I was happy to see them go. The white gauze made him look like a little mummy. He had worn the white cap all night. Physicians were hoping to identify any brain activity connected to seizures.

Those seizures frightened me so deeply. I saw them first, 24 hours earlier. I was standing by Graham's bed, feeling so good about his progress, when suddenly his right hand clenched, his knuckles turned white, and his arm drew up toward his chest. His little body tensed and shook. Both blue eyes, unfocused, fixed upward and to the right. I called the nurse, and she saw the second seizure, only seconds long. The doctor came into the room immediately and witnessed a third.

"It's a seizure," the doctor said, "It's a seizure." And the medical team transitioned to a frantic pace. Seizures were dangerous to the patients. They could cause further injury. I walked backward, away from the bed, feeling helpless, and watched the nurse hang new medications in the dispensers. I watched her shine the light into his eyes to check pupil dilation.

I was devastated—again. Up to that moment Graham had given no evidence of oxygen deprivation to his brain or any other organs in his body. Each time they checked blood gases and organ function, they gave us encouraging news. No organ in Graham's body seemed injured by lack of oxygen, despite the fact that the EMTs had not found a pulse until 30 minutes after the accident.

Things can change so suddenly.

The physician on duty, a delightful woman we all came to love, called us to the couch in Graham's room and sat down with us. "He has had a series of seizures," she told us. "They could be caused by a variety of things, but they probably indicate that the baby has suffered some brain injury." We did not speak. I heard behind me the padding feet of nurses who continued to work on Graham. "The extent of the brain injury might be determined by an MRI (magnetic resonance imaging) and an EEG," she said. "These tests were ordered immediately."

Graham's little hand drawn into a tight fist and his eyes rolled back and upward—these images troubled my heart. The doctors guessed that brain injury caused the seizures. They tried to be encouraging: "I'm not worried about seizures," one physician said to me, maybe noticing my demeanor. I probably looked like I had been run over by a truck.

"We can control seizures," he said. "We have meds that will prevent them. We can send him home with those meds. Don't worry about the seizures."

I did worry about the seizures, though. I extrapolated forward from that moment to years later. I imagined Graham trapped in a special wheelchair with his head twisted upward and his hands curled useless in his lap. Was this the future that awaited our baby boy? Had a lack of oxygen injured his brain?

The Seizures: Setback to God Knows Where

Had he lost the ability to send appropriate signals from his brain to his body?

Terrifying possibilities of permanent debilitations crowded my mind and heart. I voiced them to no one, but I could not scrub from my memory the sight of those seizures, and I could not stop the frightening march of horrible contemplations about Graham's future. I wondered what the EEG would show and what the new day would bring forth.

All night Graham had worn the electrodes. The drugs—sedatives, pain killers, and paralytics—had held him just below the surface of consciousness. His brain waves drew those squiggly lines for the EEG hour after hour.

We had already received the results of the MRI. Graham's brain looked normal to the radiologists who read such things. This confirmed the results of a CAT (computerized axial tomography) scan done the third day after the accident. These tests found no injury to Graham's brain.

All these encouraging test results faded in comparison to the actual seizures that gripped Graham's body. They might have been drug-induced, a nurse speculated. He could have been responding to severe pain, another thought. But the probable cause was obvious. Graham was the victim of a near drowning. His body had gone without oxygen for an undetermined period of time. Brain injury was the most likely culprit.

I was grateful for the optimism and attitude of the physicians. I remembered my friend Johnny in eighth grade who had asthma and was prone to hyperventilate. I had learned how to help him with his attacks, pressing a paper bag around his mouth and ordering him to blow into it. *Children can help one another,* I thought. *People in Graham's life can be taught to respond properly if he should have a seizure. I can learn what to do.* These thoughts curled like dark circles in the swirls of an uncertain future.

This is not what we hoped and prayed for Graham, the delightful boy with the endearing smile and laugh. We wanted him whole, healthy, and "normal." We wanted his brain to be perfect, his entire body and his long life in the future to be completely free of any consequences from this accident.

That is what we wanted, hoped for, and prayed for. We wanted a complete recovery. I had asked my friends and my church to pray for such an outcome. I believe that God wants to hear the desires of our hearts. That was my desire. I came to God perpetually, wringing my hands, voicing this request: "Please, God, give him a complete recovery."

I had even prayed that Graham would be better than he had been before. He had been a small newborn, low birth weight. He had been slow to crawl and diversify his vocalizations, maybe a month behind the charts. Pediatricians and geneticists had found no cause for these things.

Therapists had worked with Graham. In the weeks prior to the accident he had made amazing progress—crawling all over the house, getting into everything, even pulling up beside tables and chairs, still swaying and unsteady on his feet. We had moved the coffee table in the den into a corner so Graham would not take so many dives after pulling up.

Then he took that fateful dive into the bucket with three inches of soapy water.

I shook myself, trying to get that image out of my head, and thought of Graham playing in the den. His brother, Brady, two years older, calls him Grammy-ham. He is named Graham Russell, the middle name after my father. Graham Russell Deris was born in New Orleans almost exactly one year after Russell Bryan Crosby was buried at Restland Cemetery in Gatesville, Texas.

Our dreams for Graham Russell did not include seizures and brain injury—or a long stint in ICU. These things were detours, interruptions, we hoped. Maybe this was an interlude before the boy got back on track to become the man we dreamed he would be. Standing in the hospital room, watching them work on him, I only wanted him to live, seizures or not. We could handle seizures, like the doctor said.

That helpless feeling came over me. Things had gone wrong and there was nothing I could do. I felt an emptiness engulfing me, like my world had drowned in fear and sorrow and nothing else survived.

Pain draws life to a fine point, to a single face, one beating heart. Intellectually, we know that life is more than this single rhythm, but it does not feel that way. If that heart stops beating, the world goes dark on you.

SORROW BY THE BUCKET

The bucket sat on the driveway where the accident occurred. I could see it under the carport as I pulled on to the driveway. I climbed out of my car and snapped a picture of the bucket with my cell phone. Janet, my wife, saw me do it, and her brow wrinkled disapprovingly. She wanted the bucket destroyed, she said, and the memory of it washed from the face of the earth.

Graham's parents, Mike and Rebekah, planned an incineration ceremony for the bucket. They wanted to see it melt away into a bubbling, sizzling puddle of plastic, sent back to the liquid state from whence it came.

The bucket is not evil, I said to myself, as I held it up and looked it over. It had no intentions, good or bad. The people who made the bucket designed it to help people with ordinary tasks like washing the car. No one was negligent in designing the bucket. It held about two gallons of water, I guessed. Rebekah filled it only two or three inches deep when washing the car. The handle was green, the rest of it white. It sat flat-bottomed on the concrete, an oval shape about a foot tall. It bore no warning in pictures or words.

Some things in nature approximate a bucket—craters in rocks and holes in the ground and gourds that grow in our gardens. The portability of the bucket distinguishes it from naturally occurring reservoirs of liquid. Buckets generally come with handles. "Jack and Jill went up the hill to fetch a pail of water." The fetching of water and other things with the portable bucket has made it part of human habitations for millennia.

Buckets are designed for transporting liquid, but they can be used for many things, including a stool. Some people think the phrase *kicked the bucket* comes from medieval England where hanging victims stepped up on an inverted bucket to receive the noose.

People suffer sometimes because they are victims of persons with evil motives and intentions. Victims of crime may suffer in this way. God has granted humans an awesome and terrible freedom in giving us the ability to hurt both ourselves and others.

The suffering our family endured was not a result of evil motives or intentions. The bucket is an example of a morally neutral object. Tornadoes and tsunamis are also morally neutral. They do not arise because of human decisions or activities, as far as we know. Should theories about global climate change prove to be true, then humans may have to bear some responsibility for increasing the number and severity of natural disasters, but even still would not cause particular disasters to strike particular places and people.

Job was a rich and righteous man, the best person on the planet. His economic empire collapsed. He suffered the loss of his ten children, and all the rest of his immediate family members except for his wife. His family died in two destructive events. The first was an attack by his enemies, the Sabeans, who murdered everyone in the house and stole all the animals. The second fatal event was a "great wind" that "came from across the wilderness and struck the four corners of the house, and it fell on the young people and they died" (Job 1: 19 NKJV).

Job lost part of his family to thieves and murderers. His sorrow was complicated by the evil intentions of other people who took the lives of his loved ones.

Job lost the other part of his family to a great wind like a tornado or a hurricane. The house fell in, and all its inhabitants died. His sorrow may have been complicated by anger toward a negligent architect or builder who did not build the house per specifications, but the story does not include such information. This event is more likely viewed as a natural disaster or an act of God.

Job received the news of the death of his loved ones with sorrow. He did not seem to distinguish in his grief between those who died by the hands of men and those who died in a natural disaster.

Job also received this terrible news with unshaken faith: "Naked I came from my mother's womb, and naked shall I return there. The Lord gave, and the Lord has taken away; blessed be the name of the Lord" (Job 1:20 NKJV). The first chapter of Job concludes with this observation: "In all this Job did not sin nor charge God with wrong" (v. 22).

Job responded to God. He never blamed Satan for his troubles and sorrows. He dealt with God and dialogued with God in his emotional and mental struggles. He went straight to the Almighty, as is proper when life collapses on you and the inexplicable occurs.

Job's friends accused him of wrongdoing. "Who, being innocent, has ever perished?" asked Eliphaz, a supposed comforter to Job. "Where were the upright ever destroyed?" (Job 4:7). Eliphaz and the other comforters told Job that he was suffering because of his sins. That is how the world works, they insisted, though sometimes it seems otherwise. Ultimately, evil people suffer and good people prosper: "We have examined this, and it is true. So hear it and apply it to yourself" (5:27).

God heard the protests and pleas of Job. He answered Job with a barrage of questions: "I will question you, and you shall answer me" (Job 38:3). The first question: "Where were you when I laid the earth's foundation? Tell me, if you understand" (v. 4). "Have you ever given orders to the morning, or shown the dawn its place?" (v. 12).

Job responded this way to the questions of God: "I put my hand over my mouth" (Job 40:4). He chose to sit in silence before the mystery of God's providence.

Silence is hard for humans to endure. We want to elicit words from those who will not speak. We feel better when we are talking. But silence is sometimes the only appropriate response when confronted with the mystery and majesty of the Almighty. Sometimes you don't know whom to blame. Sometimes there is simply no one to blame, not even God.

The bucket seemed innocent and innocuous to me when I held it. It was designed to trap the water, to confine it in a small and portable space. The bucket trapped Graham in its space along with the water. Graham nearly died in that encounter. Dread and grief followed in its wake.

Children play with buckets all the time. They fill them up and tip them over. They carry water to their sandcastles and sand to their toy trucks. I have lived six decades on this earth, and I have not known another child that nearly drowned in a bucket.

THE BLAME GAME

Can we assign blame if we choose? Certainly. We can invent a thousand safer scenarios by changing the variables that led to the accident. Looking backward, practically any accident could be avoided. Safety regulations evolve in all industries on the heels of accidents. We hope that people who read of Graham's accident will be even more watchful of their children when they are playing near shallow pools and small containers. Graham was still in ICU when we heard the story of a child who drowned in a shallow puddle outside of a home.

One nurse said it was the third time in her career that she had seen such an accident with a bucket. We heard stories of children who drowned and others who nearly drowned in all kinds of situations and settings from backyards to bathtubs.

"You turn your head. It happens in an instant," said one mother, telling us how her child ingested a bottle of pills.

All of the stories were intended to give us comfort and to alleviate the crushing guilt and shame that accompanies any terrible accident, especially involving a child. The stories helped to some degree.

Rebekah was the adult in charge of Graham when the accident occurred. The weight of that responsibility overwhelmed her in those first hours. Sometimes she could not stand or talk.

She dropped her head into her lap. She wept and wept. No one could console her.

The shame and guilt Rebekah felt is known to all parents to one degree or another. In the case of Graham, a parent's worst nightmare came true. For all parents, though, guilt and self-condemnation are part of the assignment. Parenting is full of joyful opportunities and terrible responsibilities. Every parent looks back with some regret. Suffering from your own mistakes seems just. Suffering from the mistakes of another seems unjust. If a mother burns herself with the curler, she brushes it off. If she burns her child with that curler, she may suffer from some serious guilt.

No wonder God loves to forgive our sins. It's the only real cure for guilt. We stumble. We fall. We miscalculate. Something terrible happens as a result. We drown in the guilt. Even tiny slivers of responsibility end up festering in our hearts like splinters. What other real cure do we have?

Maybe we can ascribe some responsibility to the bucket. It's a bucket, after all, a human invention. The humans who made it should have done a better job, made it smaller, shorter, with a warning for parents. That helps a little, I guess, but just a little.

For the universal parental guilt there is no real cure except forgiveness. We must forgive ourselves for being imperfect parents. We must forgive our parents, too, for they were imperfect examples to us. Most of all, we must receive the forgiveness of God who alone has the authority to forgive sins.

What a relief to know that the God who made us also rescues us from our inevitable guilt. Psalm 25:17–18 expresses a prayer that every parent should learn to pray: "Relieve the troubles of my heart and free me from my anguish. Look on my affliction and my distress and take away all my sins."

The Blame Game

PRAYER IS PROPER RESPONSE

Prayer is fundamental. It is the primary spiritual discipline, talking to God.

Prayer is necessary. We must pray. Prayer itself acknowledges the presence and concern and power of God.

The presence of God is very personal in prayer. I lift my voice to God because He is present in my space in that moment. He is proximate to me. While my prayer is an affirmation of His existence and His presence in the universe, it is closer and more intimate than a theological statement that affirms this. Prayer is me whispering to God.

Prayer assumes that God cares about my predicament. I don't normally tell uncaring strangers my problems. Generally, when I open up and talk about the things that are on my heart, I am talking to someone who I believe cares about me and the things I share. Prayer is my declaration of God's concern, that His ear and His heart are turned toward me.

My prayer does not always depend upon the power of God to do something. Sometimes I want to talk to God, tell Him how things are, without any real petitions or requests. I just want Him to hear me out, to know how I feel.

When I came to God in prayer for Graham, I wanted a conversation—and more. I knew that God had the power to intervene in my grandson's life. In fact, I knew that God was the only one who could change most of the variables. Graham's survival and his health were up to God.

And I wanted God to know that I wanted Graham back, whole and healthy.

So my prayer from the hospital room was a confession of my own limitations and the limitations of every person working with Graham. We were all limited in our reach and our under-standing. We were limited in our power to change things. We were doing the various things that we could do for Graham, and doing them well and with great care. But a whole range of variables were beyond our reach, and every physician, techni-cian, and nurse knew it.

Jesus practiced prayer, and He insisted on prayer. "Jesus told his disciples a parable to show them that they should always pray and not give up" (Luke 18:1).

So I did not give up even though things looked mighty bleak. My first Facebook post after Graham's accident was from my cell phone at 6:30 the next morning. I was sitting in his room in ICU listening to the ventilator, watching the night shift trans-fer duties to the new crew. I typed with my thumbs—and prob-ably had to make ten corrections. I only type long messages when I can get to my computer and use ten digits.

The message was brief and to the point: "Graham is still critical this morning but holding his own. Pray for right lung to clear up and for no brain swelling. First three days are critical with this injury."

Rebekah had already posted something on her Facebook page, and I was receiving comments and questions from extended family and church members. I wanted to let our friends know what was happening, and I wanted people to pray for Graham.

More than 100 friends made comments on that first post. They sent our prayer request to their friends who passed it on to others. Soon we were receiving comments from people around the world who were praying for Graham.

The next morning I posted again from my phone: "Home or hospital, we are sustained by your provisions and your prayers. Got to waiting room this morning and found hot sausage biscuits delivered by the Crawfords. God is touching us thru you, his people." Almost 200 people responded on my page in some way to this post. The prayer team grew throughout the day.

PRAYER AND THE WILL OF GOD

The afternoon of the second day I explained again on Facebook the injury that Graham had sustained. Many new voices were being added to the prayers, and people wanted to know what had happened. That afternoon I asked specifically, "Please pray that Graham will return to consciousness with no significant brain injury and all his motor and cognitive functions intact. This is what we are asking God to grant us."

Bruce Nolan, a journalist from the *Baton Rouge Advocate*, quoted back to me this prayer request. "Things were so desperate," he said. "You did not know whether Graham would live or die. Yet you are asking God not just for his survival but for his complete recovery. Why?"

My response is simple: God wants to hear the petitions of our hearts. He invites us to come to Him with these requests: "In every thing by prayer and supplication with thanksgiving let your requests be made known unto God" (Philippians 4:6 KJV). This is what Jesus did: "During the days of Jesus' life on earth, he offered up prayers and petitions with fervent cries and tears to the one who could save him from death, and he was heard because of his reverent submission" (Hebrews 5:7). Jesus prayed boldly for the sick. He asked for their healing. He prayed fervently when He faced His own greatest trial.

God wants to know my heart. He wants to know what I really long for and fervently desire. I should bring that petition to Him. That is what we did with Graham. We asked for a complete recovery because that is what our hearts were longing for.

The Scripture tells us, "Let us therefore come boldly unto the throne of grace, that we may obtain mercy, and find grace to help in time of need" (Hebrews 4:16 KJV). I believe that we should come reverently and boldly to God. Being bold means to me that we ask God to grant us what we truly desire.

People everywhere began to pray this bold prayer for complete recovery for Graham even though that was not a usual outcome for this kind of traumatic injury. We prayed fervently and passionately and specifically, but we knew in our hearts that the power of prayer belongs to God, not to us. God is the one who heals. We focus our faith in Him. He is good. He is kind and compassionate. He is merciful. He is powerful. God alone was our hope.

Jesus prayed in Gethsemane before His crucifixion, "Not my will, but thine, be done" (Luke 22:42 KJV). He prayed at his time of greatest need and desperation. We do not know of a another single instance when He experienced such stress and agony.

The writer of Hebrews says that "he was heard because of his reverent submission" (Hebrews 5:7). The Father heard the prayer of His beloved Son even though Jesus still went to the Cross. That is something to contemplate when we are praying through the pain.

Notice this also: Jesus was heard because of His "reverent submission." He was completely submitted to the Father's will. Jesus knew what He wanted, and He voiced His fervent request to God: "Father, if you are willing, take this cup from me" (Luke 22:42). But even more than His sincere petition, He wanted to see the Father's will come upon this earth.

Our prayers for Graham were, in part, "Take this cup." We did not want Graham to die. That would have been the worst outcome that we could imagine, even more so than severe brain injury. At least, that is what we told ourselves in the waiting room. We just wanted him to live. We would deal with the rest. So we were sincerely saying to God, "Let the boy live, and we will deal with the consequences."

Admittedly, we did not know as we prayed those prayers what it would be like to care for a severely handicapped child. None of us had walked that road. In our hearts, though, we were ready to do so if our choices for Graham were death or severe injury. We were ready to adjust our lives to accommodate an injured Graham—at least, we thought we were when we prayed.

Our prayers also included "not my will, but Yours be done." We did not sense that our collective wills were strong enough to bring Graham through this crisis. In fact, we did not feel that the fate of Graham rested upon the quality or number of our prayers. Graham's fate was in the hands of God, and God alone.

We did not place our faith in faith itself, as far as I could see. We did not trust in our own power even through prayers. Our family did not storm heaven with the thought that we would change God's mind or change His plan for Graham. Our faith was in God alone, not our spiritual exercises or expertise. We trusted God with Graham, with ourselves, and with our future.

We confessed and believed at the time, though we could not see a way through it, that if Graham died, we would carry on with life and faith. We would still believe in the goodness of God. We would still trust in Him for our daily bread.

We could not hold God hostage. We had nothing with which to coerce God into our way of thinking. We did not try to strike deals with Him like, "God, if You spare Graham I will be a missionary to Pakistan." I cannot remember a single prayer that involved such an exchange. I do remember wishing that it was me and not Graham who was on that ventilator, and his mother said the same.

All of us who loved Graham would gladly take his place. He had lived only ten months. He was such a bright and wonderful person already, full of fun and laughter. Graham would laugh until he was exhausted while playing with his brother and sister, Brady and Mallory.

But that was not our choice. We could not take his place. We were assigned to pray for him and walk beside him through his accident to the unknown destination that awaited him and us.

We thought we were ready, and we told ourselves that we were ready, should Graham die. It was our way of praying the not-my-will-but-Thine-be-done prayer.

This dimension of our faith was greatly helped by the young mothers who sat with us in the waiting room. Holly's baby lived only 43 hours. Kristen's baby was stillborn. These women sat with us, prayed with us, and cared for us in our sorrow.

I have known Holly since she was a young teenager. She is a woman of faith, and she has a faith community that rallied around her when her baby was in trouble. They lifted up fervent prayers to God, and the baby died. Her experience with her second child ran parallel to Rebekah's experience in many ways.

Holly's presence was providential. God tempered our trust in prayer itself by having Holly come. We could not rely upon the high quality and volume of our prayers. I knew her pastor, Gary DeSalvo. We have been friends for 20 years. I know many of the people in their large, vibrant congregation. Our prayer effort would not be able to outshine theirs.

God was casting us back upon Himself through Holly. The death of her baby was a mystery that we could not unravel or fathom. We could not make comments that exalted our spirituality or maturity or faith. Every little bit of good news about Graham gave rise to praise of God. We tried to give God credit for every good thing that came our way. We did not credit humans or human activities with this miraculous work. We only gave glory to God.

We could not say in Holly's presence, "God has spared Graham because we have been faithful to Him." We knew better. Holly was faithful, too, and she did not get her miracle. We could not say, "God has seen our good lives, and He is rewarding us with Graham's healing." Holly is an obedient and faithful follower of Jesus, and she did not get her miracle.

Two statements of Jesus about prayer seem to be in tension. Sometimes they collide in our minds. Jesus said, "You may ask me for anything in my name, and I will do it" (John 14:14). He also told the Father, "Not my will, but yours be done" (Luke 22:42). The latter prayer seems for some people a way to get God off the hook.

The problem is, God is not on the hook. We cannot manipulate God into doing something that is against His will. In fact, these two prayers state the same thing from different perspectives. To ask anything in Jesus' name means that our request is consistent with the character and purpose of Jesus. That is what His name involves. The name captures the essence of the person. When I pray "in Jesus' name," I am predicating my prayer upon the essential nature of Jesus, not holding up God or making Him act regardless of His will.

Surely the will of God is a mystery. I cannot fathom it. I do not know how the will of God meshes with my own human will. I stand amazed that God has given me such wide-ranging freedom in light of His own sovereignty and providence.

I am happy to pray, to trust, and to live in this mystery concerning God's will. The Creator God has all the power in this universe—and all the answers. I have neither the power nor the answers. Hence, I walk "by faith, not by sight" (2 Corinthians 5:7).

The governor of Louisiana, Bobby Jindal, himself a person of faith, said it succinctly when I made a visit to his home just after the publication of the story about Graham in the Baton Rouge newspaper. The governor shook my hand and asked how Graham was doing. Then he said, "What a wonderful witness to the grace of God."

Now that is the summation of it: the grace of God. God is good. He gives us miracles in response to our prayers. We do not know how or when these miracles will come, but come they do. And when we get a miracle, a wonderful answer from God to our fervent prayers, we can only give Him all the praise and glory. We do not feel at all worthy to receive any of the glory. We know that God alone deserves the credit. We bow before our loving, powerful God, and we utter our thanks to Him as best we know how.

PRAYER CHANGES THINGS—AND ME

Prayer does not and cannot change the will of our great God. In fact, I do not want my prayers to change God's will. God is perfectly good and all-wise. His will is the best imaginable future for me. If I change the will of a loving God, I am sabotaging my own best future. I am always offering my prayers wisely when I quote Jesus and pray "not my will, but Yours be done."

This is why Jesus taught us to pray for God's will in the Model Prayer, the Lord's Prayer: "Thy will be done in earth, as it is in heaven" (Matthew 6:10 KJV). If God's will is done consistently in my life on this earth, then I am truly blessed, and I will achieve my highest and greatest potential.

Prayer can and does change people and circumstances. God uses our prayers in our relationships, our circumstances, and our inner life. His activities on this earth travel the channels of our prayers and soar on the wings of prayer.

Prayer is my acknowledgment of the presence of God both in this universe and in my life. To have a conversation with God is to affirm and believe to some degree that God is listening. Remember that even little faith, faith like a mustard seed, accomplishes much (Matthew 17:20). Even a prayer that begins with a contingency like, "God, if You are listening . . ." can be a powerful prayer, and it ought to be prayed.

Prayer not only acknowledges God's presence in a personal way. It also acknowledges God's concern for me and my trouble. Prayer is the confession that God cares. Everything in our spiritual lives, including prayer, rides on this truth—God is good.

Think about these two confessions that every prayer implies: God is present, God is good. Is there anything else you really need to know about life and the universe? If you believe that God is present, then you are never alone in this life. You always have the companionship of your Creator. If you believe that God is good, then you are affirming both the goodness of your present existence and the goodness of your future expectation. Your entire life is immersed in the presence and the goodness of God.

But prayer is the confession of a third reality—God is powerful. He can act in ways that no one else can act. This is what the physician was describing in his words to us during Graham's first critical hours. Humans could handle two inches of the spectrum of variables in Graham's case, from extended thumb to index finger. The rest of that spectrum, the width of outstretched arms, only God could access.

I talk to God because He is listening. He is perfectly good. He is all-powerful. If I have His ear, I am the most blessed person on the face of this earth.

The power of God is unleashed in my life through faith in Him. Our part in Graham's journey was trusting God. We petitioned God continually on Graham's behalf, knowing that our good God was listening and that He cared.

Though I cannot know exactly how our prayers worked with God's will to change things in Graham's condition and his future and to bring a miracle to pass, I know that they played a part. The Bible is full of evidence and language that indicates prayer changes things. We may integrate this truth into our theological framework in a variety of ways. But we are not permitted to deny this truth in order to accommodate our man-made framework of theology. The Word of God is our authority, not some philosophical construct.

Jesus is the One who, more than any other person in the Bible, taught us to pray with an expectation of changing the circumstances. He is the one who declared that the Father in heaven would reward us for our prayers. Although Jesus insisted that the Father knows our needs before we ask (Matthew 6:6–8), still He taught us, "Ask and it will be given to you" (Matthew 7:7).

Jesus' story of the insistent friend who needed bread teaches us that we are to be persistent in our prayers (Luke 11:5–8). He teaches this same truth in another story about a widow who demanded justice from the judge (Luke 18:1–8). The judge was reluctant to accommodate her, but he relented and met her need because she was so persistent. Jesus taught us to pray with persistence. Our Father in heaven is no reluctant judge. He will speedily answer our prayer.

Jesus asked His disciples a troubling question at the conclusion of His parable about the widow and prayer: "When the Son of Man comes, will he find faith on the earth?" (Luke 18:8). Jesus intends for us to be full of faith. He often reprimanded His disciples for their lack of faith. He teaches us to believe in God's power and providence and to ask Him boldly to meet our needs.

The blind beggar in Jericho made lots of noise (Luke 18:35–43). Jesus stopped, called out to him, and asked him what he wanted. The beggar said, "Lord, I want to see" (v. 41). Jesus knew that this blind man wanted to see, but He wanted him to say it out loud.

Now that is simple enough. Jesus asked him what he wanted, and he told Him. That is how prayer works for you and me. Jesus wants to know what we want. Our will and desires are important to Him. In fact, He is trying to shape our will and desires to match His will and desires.

Jesus concluded the exchange with this statement: "Receive your sight; your faith has healed you" (Luke 18:42). In light of this statement, we must emphasize the importance of faith in our prayers. We are to ask God for what we want believing that He cares for us and will meet our needs.

Our petition and our faith do not discount or trump the will of God. Ideally, they will be consistent with the will of God. God is shaping our hearts to make them like His own, so this will be true more and more as we mature spiritually. We will pray in a way that matches God's will. We will see our prayers answered. We will even see miracles—answers to our prayers that go beyond natural explanations.

God's question to you in your trouble is, "What do you want?" If you have already told God what you want, then tell Him again. Remember that persistence is part of prayer just like persistence is part of the Christian life, and persistence and faith are so intertwined and interconnected that they are truly hard to separate. So keep praying. Keep asking. Ask others to join you in your prayer. God answers prayer.

PRAYERS FOR A MIRACLE

Our prayer requests for Graham were posted day by day, and they were specific: pray for the right lung to be clear, pray for his foot to heal, pray for the brain not to swell, pray for no more seizures. And we prayed for a miracle, for Graham's complete recovery in every way.

No miracle God ever gave is beyond dispute. I have heard people say that they would believe if they could hear the audible voice of God from heaven. The Apostle John wrote that God spoke audibly from heaven in affirmation of Jesus (John 12:28–29). Then he recorded: "The crowd that was there and heard it said it had thundered" (v. 29). Of course they said it thundered. They did not believe. They gave a natural explanation for a supernatural event.

The same thing happened in the Resurrection of Jesus. Jesus was taken down dead from the Cross. They buried Him in a tomb. The Romans soldiers sealed it and posted a guard. Sunday morning the tomb was empty and the body of Jesus was gone. Matthew recorded that the guards were paid to say, "His disciples came during the night and stole him away while we were asleep" (Matthew 28:13). The greatest miracle in the history of humans was reduced to a matter of theft in the night.

Jesus said it would be this way. He told a story about a

beggar named Lazarus who died and went to be with Abraham in paradise and a rich man who died and went to hell (Luke 16:19–31). The rich man asked Abraham if Lazarus could be sent back to earth to warn the rich man's brothers so they wouldn't end up in hell.

Abraham said, "They have Moses and the Prophets; let them listen to them."

The rich man said, "If someone from the dead goes to them, they will repent."

Abraham responded: "If they do not listen to Moses and the Prophets, they will not be convinced even if someone rises from the dead."

And so it is. Some choose to believe in God, and they see evidence every day that God is at work in the world around them. Some choose not to believe in God, and they never see any evidence of God's work. Jesus performed miracles through the power of God, but His enemies refused to see God at work even in the compassionate miracles of Jesus (see Matthew 12:31).

Jesus told His enemies, "My Father is always at his work to this very day, and I too am working" (John 5:17). That is the perspective I want to have, and that I choose to have. I believe that God is always at work, and I see evidence of it every day.

We prayed for Graham's recovery. His brain did not swell in those first three days, and he seemed to be getting better.

The series of seizures occurred on the sixth day in PICU. We prayed that Graham would have no more seizures. The doctors speculated that those seizures could have been happening all along, but the paralytic drugs and sedatives disguised the symptoms.

The seizures prompted a flurry of activity for Graham. He was moved out of PICU for the first time in six days and transported to the MRI in another part of the hospital. During that trip he was rolled, lifted, and even "cupped" with a device designed to dislodge lung obstructions.

Graham got back from the trip precipitated by his seizures, and the doctors ordered another lung x-ray. They were shocked! His lungs were dramatically improved, particularly the right lung that had looked so cloudy in previous pictures. One physician suggested that the right lung "popped open" because of the movement and procedures initiated after the seizures.

From that moment forward Graham's progress was dramatic. With his right lung clearing up, he was weaned from the respirator and the ventilator tube was removed within a day or so.

The series of seizures, so terrifying to me, ended up precipitating events that led to dramatic improvement in Graham's health.

Doctors at first talked about weaning Graham off the increased antiseizure medications in weeks or even months. Graham demonstrated no tendency toward further seizures. The doctors at Children's Hospital decided to wean him off the antiseizure meds even before they sent him home. He received his last dosage on the day of his dismissal from the hospital. So far, we have not observed or confirmed a single seizure since that sixth day.

This is what we prayed for. This is what the medical professionals worked to accomplish. Who gets the glory? God does. He gives the answer to our prayers. If the doctors helped, that is just fine. Doctors and medicine are His gifts to us as well.

CREDIT WHERE CREDIT IS DUE

Graham's story is a great story of faith for me.

A scientist might hear this story and say, "His heart might have been beating all along, but the EMTs couldn't find the pulse."

We don't know, obviously. We know that no one found Graham's pulse for 30 minutes, including EMTs who gave him CPR at the site before they transported him. We know that his pulse was found only after he arrived at the emergency room.

We know that EMTs often have a rush of adrenaline—that their own hearts are beating fiercely in a crisis. Sometimes they find a pulse when there is none because they feel their own pounding heart rather than that of the patient. Sometimes they find no pulse for the patient in the chaos of the crisis even though the patient may have a faint one.

Rebecca, the teenager, told me that when she administered CPR in the front yard of the house, it seemed to her that Graham was still alive, that he reacted in some way to the breath she blew into him.

You know what? I don't know if Graham's pulse was too faint to detect or his heart was not beating at all. I don't know if somehow he was getting oxygen to his brain and other organs or if they were oxygen-deprived.

I do know that God spared my grandson and brought him back from the brink of death, one way or the other.

Maybe Graham returned to us because babies are resilient. They bounce back in ways that adults cannot. Maybe it is the marvelous design that God created in Graham for his own recovery that helped him survive without any injury.

Surely God used the chain of individuals who had been trained in CPR, from the teenager to the older couple to the EMTs. All of the people who touched Graham were motivated to save him, to breathe life into him. They kept working on him right up to the moment they transferred him to the emergency room physicians.

Surely God used the highly trained physicians and technicians who ministered to Graham after his arrival at the hospital. God used the medical devices and marvelous machines that are now standard equipment in emergency rooms and intensive care units. All of these fantastic tools are gifts from the Creator God who gave us minds to think and hands to work.

Graham's recovery is an ongoing story, and we are caught in the middle of it. At this point, though, it seems to be a full recovery with no apparent lingering injuries.

And that is a miracle to me, however God did it, whatever and whoever He used. I give God the glory because we are His creations, our minds are His inventions, and all the good things we produce, including the wonders of modern medicine, are ultimately His gifts.

I give God thanks for modern medicine. I am glad that Graham was minutes away from an ambulance. I give thanks that he was in the care of some of the finest physicians and nurses on earth in less than 30 minutes after the accident. I am so grateful for ventilators and miracle drugs and people who know how to use them.

I am happy that life expectancy has doubled in the last century. I am glad we are healthier than previous generations. I think this is a great gift. I am grateful every time I feel the stick of a needle in my arm. Somebody whose name I do not know will examine my blood for all kinds of problems and diseases. My doctor will get a printout of the results, and I will likely live longer and be healthier than I would have been without this astonishing science.

I give God the glory for Graham's recovery. We prayed, along with thousands of others, and God answered our prayers. Hallelujah!

SUFFICIENT GRACE

Not everybody who prays witnesses a miracle. This is fact. This is truth. What do we do when no miracle comes?

Paul asked God for a cure to some ailment that was troubling him. We speculate about it, but we do not know what it was. Paul asked the Lord three times to remove this "thorn." The Lord responded to him, "My grace is sufficient for you" (2 Corinthians 12:9). Paul adjusted his life to this answer rather than the one that he thought would relieve him of torment.

My father drowned. At least it felt that way. He couldn't breathe. He had congestive heart failure. The fluid filled up his chest, compressed his heart, and he died of suffocation.

I hated to see my dear dad die that way. He was always so robust and daring, so tuned into the present moment, so aware of God's presence, so eager for the next challenge.

Through four grueling days he made a gradual retreat from the land of the living, four days of the family's efforts to ease him with morphine, four days of hospice nurses, four days of prayers and singing around his bed, and then a merciful death.

The sharp decline started when Dad said, "It's not working, Doc." Mom drove Dad to the hospital again and again when he felt like he could no longer breathe. The doctors would drain the fluid from around his heart. He would get some temporary relief. He looked so gray and weak in those weeks before his death, in that period when he was struggling to go on, gasping for air.

My parents loaded up the car early one morning in those last days of his life when neither one of them could sleep. Dad said to Mom, "Let's go to the mountains." He always loved the mountains. Dad took us mountain climbing for recreation when we lived in El Paso. I saw those mountains every night when I laid down to sleep. From my bed I studied them, bathed in the moonlight. Orion's Belt was right above the tallest peak, framed in the open window of my bedroom.

My parents didn't tell anyone what they were planning. We children would have insisted they stay at home, close to the hospital and doctors. Mom called from Fort Stockton, already 200 miles from home and heading west. I really thought that she would have to deal with Dad's death on the road.

Dad and Mom had their last fling together, as it turned out. They always loved to drive the roads of these United States. By the time I was 16 years old, I had watched the world whiz by in 27 of the states. They took off together, Dad at death's door, stayed with friends in El Paso one night, then headed to Cloudcroft, New Mexico, to see the snow-covered peaks. Dad had avoided high altitudes for years because of his difficulty breathing, but he urged Mom on to the heights. They stayed for some hours, surveying the beautiful scenery of the southern Rockies, then turned the car back toward home. They were gone only 48 hours or so.

They got back, went to the hospital, and started hospice care.

I did not realize how difficult it would be for me to make Dad comfortable rather than better. When his breathing grew labored, we did not take him to the hospital to drain the fluid. For a few seconds, I did not understand. I processed "hospice" again, grappling with the concept. It dawned on me then the full import of our decision. We were going to let Dad die.

I was angry for some time, arguing within my own spirit about this course of action we had chosen—and Dad had chosen. Dad was the one who told the doctor that the treatments were not helping. Dad was the one who first received the suggestion of hospice. I guess I was angry at him as well.

I heaved a sigh of resignation, finally, and helped Dad to his feet for a futile attempt to urinate. His body was not processing fluids. He was miserable, as was I.

RESPOND TO SORROW WITH SONG

We gave Dad morphine, and it eased his anxiety and relaxed his breathing. I adjusted my expectations to the reality of Dad's impending death, and we began to sing the songs of our faith.

We grew up singing because Dad and Mom loved to sing. Dad created a gospel quartet with his four oldest sons. I was 11 years old. He told me I was going to sing. I said, "No, I can't sing, and I don't want to sing."

Dad said, "David, you are going to sing bass. I will teach you." Under protest, I began to sing the bass line an octave higher in hymns and songs, mostly Southern gospel. Tom sang the lead, Dan the baritone, and Tim the tenor. We sang a capella, listening to one another, working on harmonies.

We sang and sang together for more than a decade, in 300 different churches, and when Dad was dying, we gathered around his bed and sang some more—for hours and hours. Someone would strike up a tune, and everyone would join in. We did not need hymnals. We knew by heart the words and the harmonies to hundreds of songs.

We surrounded my father with a continual chorus as he died. The songs were full of new meaning as we sang them in those hours when Dad lingered between heaven and earth. I realized then how much the poetry of faith was really about suffering and dying and going to heaven, being with God. Every word seemed underlined, emphasized.

We took turns weeping. If I lost my composure, still the song continued, carried forward by others who still had their voices.

We responded to Dad's death by singing the songs that were dear to him, that he had taught us to sing. They were the finest comfort in those hours. We sang them together in four-part harmony. They became our own words.

Singing requires exertion. If you really sing, you have to reach way down inside, like Dad said. You have to force that song upward from your diaphragm. You have to breathe deeply, work those muscles. It takes some energy to really sing.

Dad could not sing when he was weak, when his breath left him. He could talk softly, but he could not sing. We sang for him when he was too weak to sing. That is how we carried him along when he was dying, how we carried ourselves along.

Mother lay down beside Dad. She picked out songs. She quoted passages of Scripture when the singing hit a lull, whole chapters from the Psalms that she had memorized recently or years ago. Some of those passages we all knew because, along with singing, they had taught us the Scriptures both in concept and by rote memory.

The Scriptures and songs came back to bless us at the memorial service. First Baptist Church of Gatesville, Texas, was packed that cold day in December 2011. Dad and Mom had planned the entire service together. Two people alternated in reading all 58 verses of 1 Corinthians 15, the Apostle Paul's most important discourse on the Resurrection and our own future after death. A family friend of many years, the Rev. Jerry Walters, brought a message about salvation through faith in Christ, just as Dad wanted.

We followed the custom in central Texas, opening the coffin at the end of the service. We sang as people passed by to pay their last respects, to see Dad's physical body for the last time. For maybe 30 minutes the family sang, more than a hundred of us at that time, and others joined in, too, who knew Dad and knew the songs.

We broke into song at the cemetery, standing by the grave. It was cold with a biting wind, but we stood around the grave and held one another close. My brother Tim said a few words and quoted some Scripture, and then we lifted up our voices to God, soprano, alto, tenor, and bass. These were songs about heaven, songs that came to our minds and hearts when the grave was still open, a tribute to Dad, a statement of our faith in God.

The songs expressed what we knew to be true in faith: Dad was in the presence of God and fully healed. He was in a place where no sickness or pain could enter. We sang this truth and tried to hold firmly to it as we buried Dad.

We carry those songs forward still, in our minds and hearts. When we gather as a family we always sing together. My world has been full of songs of faith since Dad said to me, "You are going to sing."

Dad's death still troubles me years later. Dad lived his faith so powerfully, with such adventure and daring. He should have died peacefully without pain, it seems to me, like Aunt Monnie died, and my father-in-law, Jack Hamilton.

But Dad didn't go that way. He suffocated slowly over the course of hours and days. I ask God why sometimes, why my father had to suffer such a miserable death. I have told God repeatedly that I don't want to die that way. Nobody does.

The answers have not come to me. This, too, is a mystery. I must entrust these questions to God—over and over again. I don't get answers. I don't understand. I just trust.

> *"Be careful for nothing; but in every thing by prayer and supplication with thanksgiving let your requests be made known unto God. And the peace of God, which passeth all understanding, shall keep your hearts and minds through Christ Jesus"* (Philippians 4:6–7 KJV).

SUFFERING IS CERTAIN

We are oriented toward comfort and prosperity culturally and theologically. If we are suffering, we assume that we are outside of the will of God. Pain means we are doing something wrong.

This is not the Bible's view of suffering. The Bible does not say that good people will always be comfortable. It says the opposite. Good people often suffer.

Jesus of Nazareth is the perfect illustration of this truth. He began His life in obscurity, without even a house in which to be born. As a boy He became a political refugee living in Egypt. He died a miserable death at an early age.

Jesus came into this world to suffer. He was a "man of sorrows," as Isaiah described Him, "familiar with suffering" (Isaiah 53:3 GW). In Isaiah's prophecy the Messiah is God's "suffering servant." Jesus interpreted His mission in large part from the Book of Isaiah. He announced His mission in His hometown by quoting Isaiah 61:1–2, one of Isaiah's "servant songs" (see Luke 4:18–19).

Peter and the other disciples reacted negatively to Jesus' statement that He must suffer and die. "Never, Lord!" Peter said emphatically. "This shall never happen to you!" (Matthew 16:22). Jesus told Peter that he was thinking in human terms rather than seeing things from a heavenly perspective. He went on to tell them that they were sure to suffer as His disciples. He gave them one His most famous sayings: "Whoever wants to save their life will lose it, but whoever loses their life for me will find it" (Matthew 16:25).

Jesus said, "Blessed are you when people insult you, persecute you and falsely say all kinds of evil against you because of me" (Matthew 5:11).

Jesus taught us that trouble is inevitable: "In this world you will have trouble. But take heart! I have overcome the world" (John 16:33).

This theme of suffering and serving was difficult for the disciples to integrate into their concept of the Promised One, the Messiah. They saw the Messiah as a great leader who would bring them victory in the battles against their enemies. The Messiah, in their view, would reestablish Israel as the center of the world. This is the reasoning behind their final question for the Lord Jesus before His ascension: "Lord, are you at this time going to restore the kingdom to Israel?" (Acts 1:6). Jesus turned their attention from a focus upon the triumph and victory at the end of the age to the task at hand—giving witness to all the world of the good news of forgiveness.

I wonder if the suffering of Jesus was the reason Judas betrayed Him. Maybe Judas was expecting a great military general who would lead them all to victory. Instead, Jesus was going to the Cross. Perhaps Judas gave up on Jesus as Messiah for this reason and sold Him out. Suffering just did not fit with his view of God's promise.

People still do this today. They suppose that their faith should protect them from suffering. Instead, after trusting in

Jesus as Messiah and Savior, they experience the hardship and trouble that He promised would come. Their faith is shaken because they misunderstood.

Paul described our present troubles in this way:

> *"Though outwardly we are wasting away, yet inwardly we are being renewed day by day. For our light and momentary troubles are achieving for us an eternal glory that far outweighs them all. So we fix our eyes not on what is seen, but on what is unseen, since what is seen is temporary, but what is unseen is eternal"* (2 Corinthians 4:16–18).

Our troubles do not seem to us to be "light and momentary." They seem very weighty and long-lasting. In fact, our sorrows become deeper and longer than we ever dreamed they would. We hear the terms "light" and "momentary," and we suppose that this describes a Christian's troubles in light of culture and neighbors. We assume that we will have troubles, but that our troubles will not be so weighty or sorrowful or of such long duration as those who do not trust in Christ.

We discover differently. If not yet, then soon, if you live long enough, your troubles will test you to the very core of your being. You will experience pain that is indescribable and sorrow that is unassailable. It will last far longer and be far more intense than you ever dreamed any trouble would be. Life will take you into its graduate school of pain.

The Apostle Paul had troubles of that nature. He lists them in a couple of places—beatings, imprisonment, shipwreck, hunger, even stoning (see 2 Corinthians 11:22–33). But with the adjectives "light and momentary," he is describing our current troubles in the light of our eternal home in heaven. These present problems, so urgent and painful, will one day seem insignificant compared to the wonders that God has waiting for us.

Our faith in God does not insulate us from trouble. It helps us to be faithful to God through the trouble.

We love God and trust Him because He is God and deserves our love and trust. He is faithful and compassionate toward us. He demonstrated the full extent of His love by sending His one and only Son to die on the Cross for our sin. In response, we want to bring Him glory with our lives. We want to obey His commands and follow Him.

Our love for God and our obedience to His commands are without any contingency. We do not withhold our love or obedience when times are difficult or trouble comes our way. We do not question God's goodness and His faithfulness in the midst of suffering. Instead, we give Him praise even when our pain and sorrow seem more than we can bear. Like Paul and Silas, we break into song at midnight despite the ordeal through which we have passed (Acts 16:25).

GRATITUDE IS ALWAYS A PROPER RESPONSE

I heard Darrell praising God again, thanking Him for all his blessings. Darrell has a quick smile and many friends. He is pleasant to be around.

He lives at the Jefferson Healthcare facility, a nursing home filled with people in wheelchairs. When we have Bible studies there, our people scatter out and wheel the worshippers from their rooms to the meeting.

I met Darrell when I was conversing with his roommate, a man who seemed unable to believe in God. His roommate left this life soon after our visit. As far as I know, he never believed.

Darrell, on the other hand, continues to trust God day by day, living in a spirit of gratitude and praise. You would wonder how he does it if you saw him. He has no feet, and one of his hands is gone. The other hand is just a twisted stump with two or three almost useless digits.

One day we were having a worship service at the nursing home, and the leader gave us an opportunity to thank God for something in our lives. People expressed gratitude for family members and friends and caregivers.

Then Darrell spoke up from his wheelchair turned toward the crowd. He wanted to thank God for heaven. When he got to heaven, he said, gesturing with a stump, he would have his hands and his feet again. He would be healthy and whole for all eternity. Disease and misfortune had stolen his hands and feet in this life, but for Darrell that was just "light and momentary" affliction compared to the glory that would one day be revealed in him.

Our gratitude as believers is not anchored to or dependent upon our present circumstances. Whatever the current state of affairs, we give thanks. Thanksgiving is a life orientation, a fundamental perspective of faith. It begins and ends in the character of God and His forever promises sealed in the sacrifice of Christ.

Ingratitude is a terrible sin, and it only makes things worse. It interjects bitterness into our sorrow and resentment into our pain. It is listed among the worst sins that people can commit: "For although they knew God, they neither glorified him as God nor gave thanks to him" (Romans 1:21). "People will be lovers of themselves, lovers of money, boastful, proud, abusive, disobedient to their parents, ungrateful, unholy" (2 Timothy 3:2).

Jesus described the amazing love of God in His teachings and His stories. He said that we should love our enemies if we wanted to follow God because God is kind even to those who are ungrateful (Luke 6:35).

We are under obligation to give God thanks. He has given us all things to enjoy. Every breath, every beat of our hearts is a gift from him. We are indebted to Him both for our existence and our daily sustenance. Christ upholds all things, including us, by the word of His power (Hebrews 1:3).

Many times we do not know the specific will of God for certain matters and decisions. We pray and follow our best judgment in view of His character and His work in our lives. But we do have clear statements about the will of God in many matters, and one of them is this: "Give thanks in all circumstances; for this is God's will for you in Christ Jesus" (1 Thessalonians 5:18).

AN INVITATION TO SUFFERING

Jesus took the difficult path of suffering because it was the right way to go. He did not relish the pain. Like all humans, He withdrew from the pain. Theologians have postulated a variety of explanations for Jesus' prayer in Gethsemane, "Let this cup pass from me" (Matthew 26:39 ESV). I think the prayer expresses the natural and necessary human instinct to avoid pain.

Jesus submitted to the will of the Father. His assignment was completed in His suffering.

Medical professionals who work in PICU will have their hearts broken, that's for sure. Not everyone gets a miracle when a child is sick or injured. And nothing is more devastating than losing a child.

The physicians and nurses who perpetually hovered around Graham were highly trained and highly skilled. They knew how to read the monitors and charts and operate the machines. They understood when medications were to be administered. They treated Graham with care that was intensive for Graham and intensive for them. They did so hour after hour and day after day.

Christen was one of the intensive care nurses appointed to watch over Graham. She told me about the heartache that came with her job, the sorrow that she observed in families daily and felt in her own soul as well. Graham's miraculous recovery was a message from God to her, she said. It affirmed her in this difficult profession she had chosen, and it helped her see in a new way that God was at work in PICU even when the results were not what everyone hoped and prayed for. She requested a picture with miracle Graham. We snapped it in the corridor just outside of PICU before we left, Christen hugging him close and Graham looking like the miracle he is.

Who would choose this profession? I wondered as I watched that PICU team work. They were set up for great disappointment and heartache. They had to have a special calling to show up on that floor and unit knowing the pain and sorrow they would see. Yet they did it day after day. It was enough for them to relieve the suffering with a special medication or procedure. It was enough for them to work for and celebrate a good day today for the little patient even though tomorrow might be miserable.

If we are going to help people in trouble and sorrow, then we must cultivate the spirit of gratitude toward God that remains steady even if the rewards, along with the troubles, are only light and momentary. Doctors cannot heal every patient. Counselors cannot fix every mental and emotional problem. Children cannot keep their parents alive forever, no matter how good their care. The cup of cold water must be enough to keep the caregiver going. If today we can bring a little relief to the pain and sorrow, then it has been a good day.

Sometimes we distance ourselves from suffering and sorrow. We move as far away from it as possible. We avoid hospitals and nursing homes. We avoid seeing sick people in any setting. We don't know what to do for them, and we don't know what to say to them.

We are making a poor choice when we try to excise sorrow and sickness from our environs. We are missing one of God's great blessings.

Suffering and sorrow, when handled with faith, help shape us and make us more like Jesus. Jesus Himself was perfected through the suffering that He endured (Hebrews 5:8). Our suffering produces the same result if we respond in faith. We should position ourselves among those who mourn and mourn with them. We do not need strategies or explanations or even words. We can be present with them in silence. It means a lot to those who suffer just to know that they are not alone. Our presence means we are shouldering a little bit of the sorrow on their behalf.

Sometimes we choose the path of suffering. We have not lost our minds. We are doing what honors God.

Foster parents often do this. They choose the path of suffering. They intend to cultivate and express deep concern and love for the children in their care. They know that those children will likely be returned to their families one day, and they will have to let go. I have seen their love for the children, and I have seen their sorrow when they are gone.

They choose to do this work despite the sorrow and grief involved.

Jesus told the story of the good Samaritan in part so we would understand the cost of loving someone the way He calls us to love them. The love of God will make you choose to walk into a trial. You know it will be trouble and heartache to take that path, yet you do it anyway.

Love will make you give more of yourself than you intended, more than others would suggest you give. Your love for others will cost you. You will become deeply invested in them as you give of yourself. In binding up their wounds and helping them to their feet, you will connect your life to theirs, and you will feel more pain when they leave as a result. Every caregiver knows this to be true. The more deeply you love, the more deeply you grieve.

Some people harden their hearts against such connection. They think this will protect them from sorrow and loss. They choose not to love or care. They have been hurt before, perhaps, and the cost of love seems too great.

If we respond to sorrow and loss by trying to insulate ourselves from further pain, we actually amplify the sorrow. We create an unhealthy solitude. We live solo in a way that we were never intended to live, a way that may create alienation and even despair.

People were made to be in relationships. The deeper those relationships go, the greater quality of life we experience. Genuine, wonderful living is the result of loving relationships. Abundant life happens in the arc between my heart and the one I love.

To open your heart to love is to open it to sorrow. Inevitably, we lose the ones we love, but to live without love is the greatest sorrow of all.

Therefore Jesus taught us to resist the temptation to protect and insulate ourselves from loving relationships. He taught us to do the opposite—to pour out our lives on behalf of others: "Whoever wants to save their life will lose it, but whoever loses their life for me will find it" (Matthew 16:25). He told us to take up our cross daily. This means we are to live a life of self-surrender—receiving whatever pain may be involved so that the love of Christ may be revealed through us.

NOT CHOOSING YOUR POISON, BUT CHOOSING YOUR ANTIDOTE

People use the phrase *choose your poison* to suggest that pain or death is inevitable, but you can choose the instrument or avenue of your pain. That may be true in a limited way, but it is not true in a general way. We do not choose, as a general rule, the diseases that will afflict us or the accidents that will injure us or the enemies that will attack us.

We choose the antidotes, not the poison. We choose our response to the diseases, injuries, and betrayals that come our way.

The pain in our lives changes us, not just because it happens, but because it requires a response. We always respond to pain. Physically, we grimace or cry out when we hurt. Emotionally, we respond with disappointment or anger or despair.

Our responses to pain change us in fundamental ways. This is easily observed all around us. People make adjustments to the troubles that beset them. Sometimes those adjustments are sweeping changes that usher in a whole new life.

I return to this writing task after attending the funeral of Terry, a man about my age. Terry received the news that he had cancer. He received the test results that showed it to be inoperable and terminal. And he died, all within a two-week span.

Terry and his family did not have a choice about this disease. They do not know where it came from or why it struck him so fiercely. Now he is gone from this life, and they are left to adjust to the new realities that confront them.

Searching for an answer to the question *why* is important and necessary. On a grand scale, the philosophers and theologians will continue to make their search and refine their theories. On a personal level, it is inevitable that we will look for this answer as well. "Why do bad things happen?" I have asked this many times.

LOVE IS THE GREATEST RESPONSE

I have my own simple theory about why there is pain and suffering in the world. I think it has to do with the nature of love.

Love is the highest good in human experience, some would say, including Jesus of Nazareth, who identified love of God and neighbor as the greatest commandments.

Love in its highest expression must be freely given to be genuine. It cannot be coerced or programmed. Love in its purest form is bound to the will. It is a moral choice. Hence God gives us the command to love. He does not command us to breathe. Breathing is programmed into the very core of the nervous system. But He does command us to love. Love is a choice, an activity of a higher order—the highest order.

The capacity to freely love another being is the highest form of moral expression known to us. This particular dimension of being human we see as divine. We are made in the image of God and therefore able to love God and one another.

God gives His love freely to us. God is the very center of moral choice in the universe. He is perfectly free, and He chooses to love perfectly.

Made in His image, humans are given this precious gift, the choice to love. It is a fearsome capacity, this freedom to love, for the gift itself can only be given along with the terrible possibility of rejection. I am free to love only if I am also free not to love.

And life without love is the flipside of God's life, His essential being. A moral agent is one who has the capacity to love. Should he choose not to love, he turns his will and moral agency against all that honors God and brings Him pleasure.

Perhaps humans are not the first created beings in this universe to receive the gift of moral agency. The Bible indicates there was another long ago who received such a gift. Isaiah 14:12–15 has for centuries been understood with a double meaning. It describes an earthly king who refused the way of love, and it may also describe our ancient foe, Satan, who also refused the love of God.

Satan is real, the Bible teaches. He is the personal presence of evil in our world, an evil that is aggressive, not passive. He turned against the love of God long ago, and he was present on this planet when humans arrived. Satan, the devil, embodies the rebellion against God's love. When we join that rebellion, we are in league with him.

The presence of Satan, a being of high order who refused the love of God, accounts for some of the evil in the world. Our own moral choices that defy God's love account for much of the suffering and pain that we and those around us experience.

The natural order, the ecosystem of which we are a part, is configured by our Creator in such a way as to enable our moral freedom. Moral qualities like discipline and honesty affect our work and relationships, and moral choices change the way the ecosystem operates. A greedy man may dam the creek and create a lake on his own property while damaging the farming operations of the people downstream. A loving man may clear every obstruction in the creek to make certain that the water reaches his neighbors. We all live downstream from someone physically, emotionally, and spiritually.

This is my attempt to explain natural disaster. What we perceive as random and evil events in the natural order—hurricanes and cancers—are somehow essential to the expression of moral freedom, and the high value of moral freedom is itself the explanation of why God made this particular world rather than another.

I am content with my personal reasoning about good and evil, about the world, the flesh, and the devil, and I am content to hold my opinions lightly. I do not know for sure where all the evil comes from, but I know so little anyway. For me to grasp the origin of evil in the world would certainly be a miracle.

My simple explanation is centered upon love. I think love is the heart of the teaching and example of Jesus. I think it is the finest and most faithful avenue for addressing our relationship to the world as His followers. Choosing to love is the key to being like our Lord in this world.

Jesus Himself summed up the path we are to take: "A new command I give you: Love one another. As I have loved you, so you must love one another. By this everyone will know that you are my disciples, if you love one another" (John 13:34–35).

Living a life of love is the best way on this planet to enhance the good and combat the evil. A life of love faithfully represents our Savior who loved us to this extent—that He laid down His life.

Love is the choice that brings God glory. When I choose to love, I am demonstrating my connection to God and my knowledge of God: "Everyone who loves has been born of God and knows God. Whoever does not love does not know God, because God is love" (1 John 4:7–8).

Love is the greatest response of all to the suffering and heartache in the world and in our lives. Giving and receiving love helps heal the hurts that life delivers to our bodies and our spirits.

Love God with all your heart when sorrow comes your way. Make love of God your first confession: "I love the Lord" (Psalm 116:1). Remember in your sorrow that God loved you first and that His love is the prototype.

Love one another more intensely. Confess love for others more freely when sorrow comes. Serve each other when pain is debilitating. Express your love in all the practical ways that minimize the sorrow and enhance the joy.

Give yourself with abandon to this life of love. Leave behind the behaviors, dreams, and goals that contradict love or stand in its way. Make love the supreme expression of your life every day.

The evil that discourages you—and sometimes overwhelms you—will seem less daunting and fearful as you love. Reach out to lift the one who has fallen near you. The fact that the fallen are everywhere will recede in your mind as the one before you stands up again. You will both be ready to face another day for having shared the moment of love.

This path of love is not sentimental or fanciful. It is not the embrace of an illusion or the expression of weakness. Love is the essential nature of the Creator God. It is fundamental to our lives and to this universe. Loving God and neighbor is a participation in the life of God, and that is the only real life there is.

We withdraw and recoil from pain as a reflex. This protects us from injury. Withdrawal, however, is not a healthy way to live in the world. To withdraw is to make the choice that opposes love. We think it will protect us, pulling back into ourselves and erecting the barricades, but in the end it afflicts us and compounds all our sorrows.

Our pain demands attention. If it is perpetual, it may collapse our life upon itself. Withdrawal may seem the way to manage and control our pain, but Jesus does not recommend it. "In this world you will have trouble," Jesus told His disciples. "But take heart! I have overcome the world!" (John 16:33).

Find somebody to love when life turns on you.

We are all wounded in the journey of life. Trouble comes our way. We combat the feelings of discouragement and despair that creep over us in the middle of trouble by finding somebody to love. People in need are our neighbors. They are nearby. They may not look like us. That is OK. The Samaritan loved across racial and religious lines. If we learn to love not only our neighbor but also our enemy, we will be loving like God loved us.

Love a Muslim or Buddhist or atheist. Love someone different than you. Love an immigrant. God loves those who are ungrateful for all the blessings of life. You follow God when you love those who have hurt you, persecuted you, and done you evil. If you do them good, then you are being like your Father in heaven. He sends His rain on the just and the unjust.

Love in simple, practical ways. *Love* is a verb more so than a noun. It is motion more than emotion. Love with a cup of cold water, a visit to the hospital or nursing home. Get up from the couch. Put on your walking shoes. Get out of yourself and into your world. As you love those around you, your pulse will quicken, your head will rise, your shoulders will straighten, and your heart will feel better.

Nobody is more hopeful about their community and their world than those who are working to make it a better place every day. Love pours us out, uses us up, and lays us down in the most beautiful way. Love is the energy of our spirit turned toward God: "The only thing that counts is faith expressing itself through love" (Galatians 5:6).

SUFFERING ENCOUNTERED AND ADDRESSED

Jesus told the story of the good Samaritan in answer to the question, "Who is my neighbor?" (Luke 10:25–29). The man who asked the question was uncomfortable with his own performance on the Second Commandment, "Love your neighbor as yourself." He wanted to justify himself by narrowly defining the meaning of the word *neighbor*. We all want to do this.

Truly, our problem with the Great Commandment is not the first part, "Love God," but the second part, "love your neighbor." Loving God is subjective and internal, we feel. If we are faithful in our prayers, devotions, and worship, however we practice these things, we feel that we are loving God.

No, the Second Commandment is the one that gets to us. Sometimes we just turn away and go on with life. Who can really love their neighbor as they love themselves?

If we are determined to keep the commandment, we take a hard look at it. We check every word in it. We want to get the proper meaning, the full meaning. The Second Commandment stumps us. It makes us feel uncomfortable, like we are not measuring up.

Jesus explained love of neighbor by describing a man who turned aside to help a victim of crime lying beside the road. Two religious professionals, a Levite and a Pharisee, had already passed by the man. The Samaritan, part of a group of people who were despised by the Jews, stopped to help the man who had been beaten and robbed. He poured wine and oil on the man's wounds and bandaged them. He placed the man on his own donkey and took him to the inn and took care of him overnight. The next day he gave the innkeeper money to cover whatever expenses he might further incur in helping the man. "Look after him," the Samaritan said. "When I return, I will reimburse you for any extra expenses you may have."

Who does this? Who can afford to do this? The further the story goes, the more unlikely it becomes that anyone will be able to fulfill the command of love. I get to the end of the story and think, "I can't do this. I don't know anyone who can." The process is so lengthy and expensive, and the world is so full of the beaten and robbed, my whole life would be overcome with helping the wounded neighbor.

Then the truth dawns on me. I do know someone who loves like this. His name is Jesus. He rescued me when I was fallen, unable to help myself. He came to me, bandaged me up, and took me where I could not go by myself. He paid the whole bill.

The story of the good Samaritan is an autobiography. Jesus is the good Samaritan who alone loves like this. He expended Himself completely in the work of our rescue from guilt and shame. He loves us just like this. "This is love: not that we loved God, but that he loved us and sent his Son as an atoning sacrifice for our sins" (1 John 4:10). I look around me, and I wonder, *Where is Jesus in this world?* I want to see His activity and try to follow in His footsteps.

I have seen the footprints of Jesus. They leave the house of worship and disappear into the mist of pain and suffering in this world. If you follow those footprints into the pain and sorrow in your community, you will find Jesus there, bending over the wounded, binding up their wounds, waiting on you.

The Second Commandment redirects your inquiring mind, as God intended it should. If you take it seriously and try to live it out, you move your focus from the knotty perplexities regarding the origin of evil in this world. Instead, the commandment shifts your focus to a more personal and even more unsettling question: Given your gifts and abilities, what are you doing to help your neighbor in need?

The tragedy of this question is that our love for neighbor is often truly pitiful if not absent altogether. We find ourselves in the same shape as the man who asked Jesus, "Who is my neighbor?" in an attempt to justify himself. Everybody gets slammed on this one.

The unbounded joy of this question is that I can do something about it, something very practical and immediate. I can reach out to the widow, the orphan, the prisoner, and the poor. I can seek with all my heart to love the suffering and hurting people around me.

If I choose this path, my life is suddenly endowed with new relationships that continually reward me. Contrary to what I imagined, needy people have a lot to give. I am enriched by every neighbor I try to bless from the hospital to the local school.

I replace the continual complaint and disturbance of the question without answer: "Why?" I have a new question that gets me out of bed every morning, lifts my chin, straightens my shoulders, and launches me into the new day.

And the new question is: "How? How can I love somebody in need today?" I feel a spring in my step and hope in my heart as I leave my home and enter a world full of trouble—and full of opportunities to love.

New Hope® Publishers is a division of WMU®, an international organization that challenges Christian believers to understand and be radically involved in God's mission. For more information about WMU, go to wmu.com. More information about New Hope books may be found at NewHopeDigital.com. New Hope books may be purchased at your local bookstore.

Use the QR reader on your
smartphone to visit us online at
NewHopeDigital.com

If you've been blessed by this book, we would like to hear your story. The publisher and author welcome your comments and suggestions at: newhopereader@wmu.org.